"Twitter and Facebook and Blogs, Oh My! In this bewildering new field of social media, Mergel and Greeves expertly provide practical advice for governments to harness the power of these new online services."

—Bill Schrier, deputy director, Center for Digital Government, eRepublic.com; Former CTO (CIO) City of Seattle

"This is simply a must-read book for anyone interested or involved with social media in the public sector. The authors take a refreshing and original approach supported by excellent examples regarding the evolving role social media is playing and can play in government. Having worked with and known both Mergel and Greeves, I cannot think of two better-experienced authors to help guide us through the new realities of social media in government."

—Dr. Alan R. Shark, executive director, Public Technology Institute and assistant professor Rutgers University School of Public Affairs & Administration

"In the local government sector there seem to be three schools of thought regarding social media: 'I've got a Facebook page—let's jump right in!' 'Not happening on my watch!' and 'Who cares?' This field guide is perfect for any of the above, as it provides practical applications and rationale for why local government needs to connect with people where they are—which is on the internet. Our association of nearly 500 innovative local governments knows that Mergel and Greeves are the perfect authors for this must-have tutorial. Greeves collaborates with us as a top notch trainer and both of these authors know the topic very well."

—Karen Thoreson, president and chief operating officer, Alliance for Innovation

"As the poet LL Cool J once said, there is a difference between doing it and doing it well. The same is true with the use of social media in government—there can be a stark divide between agencies dabbling in it and those agencies executing well. 10,000 fans/followers vs. 100. Fifteen comments and RTs vs. an empty ghost town. Driving real mission results vs. being a gimmick. If you ask most senior leaders in government, they understand the need to be in social media but they don't know how to do it well. Instead they leave it to an intern and end up with an unsuccessful program. Every day on GovLoop.com, our network of 60,000 government leaders, people share best practices and ask questions of social media in government. I've often been asked by members of a good reference book to get going for their federal, state, or local government social media programs. I never had an answer—now I do! This field guide is the go-to resource to ensure your social media programs deliver real mission results. Mergel and Greeves are experts in the field—a blend of research and real-world experience to get you to where you need to go."

—Steve Ressler, founder and president of GovLoop.com

Social Media in the Public Sector
Field Guide

Social Media in the Public Sector Field Guide

DESIGNING AND IMPLEMENTING STRATEGIES AND POLICIES

Ines Mergel and
Bill Greeves

JOSSEY-BASS
A Wiley Imprint
www.josseybass.com

Cover image: Ines Mergel
Cover design: J. Puda

Published by Jossey-Bass
A Wiley Imprint
One Montgomery Street, Suite 1200, San Francisco, CA 94104-4594—www.josseybass.com

Jossey-Bass books and products are available through most bookstores. To contact Jossey-Bass directly call our Customer Care Department within the U.S. at 800-956-7739, outside the U.S. at 317-572-3986, or fax 317-572-4002.

Wiley publishes in a variety of print and electronic formats and by print-on-demand. Some material included with standard print versions of this book may not be included in e-books or in print-on-demand. If this book refers to media such as a CD or DVD that is not included in the version you purchased, you may download this material at http://booksupport.wiley.com. For more information about Wiley products, visit www.wiley.com.

Library of Congress Cataloging-in-Publication Data

Library of Congress Cataloging-in-Publication Data has been applied for and is on file with the Library of Congress.

ISBN 978-1-118-10993-9 (paper); ISBN 978-1-118-47274-3 (ebk.); ISBN 978-1-118-42375-2 (ebk.); ISBN 978-1-118-42372-1 (ebk.)

Printed in the United States of America
FIRST EDITION
PB Printing   10 9 8 7 6 5 4 3 2 1

CONTENTS

FIGURES AND TABLES

FIGURES

TABLES

PREFACE

Perhaps social media have not been with us long enough to be called universal just yet. But there is little question that they have had a profound impact on our culture, communication, and lifestyle. Governments can no longer scoff and dismiss them as a technology fad. Social media, with their varied faces and myriad uses, have woven themselves firmly into the fabric of our daily lives.

But how do government agencies find the "right" way to capitalize on the explosive growth of social media and put these tools to work on achieving government missions? And how can agencies make it happen despite the lighter wallets and heavier workloads they are all facing today? These are the types of questions that we have wrestled with ourselves.

Through her scholarly pursuits, Ines became captivated by the ways in which government has found unique applications of social media. By the time we began writing this book, she was already a recognized thought leader on the topic of social media in government and had crafted her courses at Syracuse University around the integration of technology into the process of civic discourse and citizen engagement. Meanwhile, Bill was on a path that led him to similar interests. As a government technology practitioner, he was passionate about the ever-increasing potential of social media as an entirely new platform from which to deliver government services and seek feedback from the varied audiences served by government agencies.

Fate, or more accurately social media, brought us together during a series of captivating online conversations focused on the noticeable lack of social media guidance for government agencies. Early on, we recognized that we had a tremendously passionate and creative group of peers both in higher education and in government agencies who had already seen beyond the basics of social media and were elevating the visibility and usability of these tools in government. But what about the rest of our peers? How could we help the vast majority of our government peers who did not yet see or believe in this potential? Could we work together to gather, organize, and communicate the value of social media using a casual and easy-to-follow approach? Our answer was a confident yes!

ABOUT THIS BOOK

This Field Guide is the companion to *Social Media in the Public Sector: A Guide to Participation, Collaboration, and Transparency in the Networked World*, authored by Ines Mergel. This book is designed for the social media neophyte. It is not a textbook. It is not a heavy theoretical dissertation or a classroom reference. It is instead designed to be a field guide—a melding of the *what*, the *why*, and the *how* of social media in government. We've stocked it with real-life examples and case studies from your government peers. You do not need to read this book from cover to cover before you start your own experimentation with social media. You can skip around and pull out the parts that are relevant to your own organization and your objectives. We've done our best to keep things relevant and easy to apply to your own needs.

The book is divided into four main parts. In Part One, we focus on the history and evolution of social media. What are they and where did they come from? How do they differ from traditional media? How did they become such a common aspect of so many people's lives? Why do governments need to pay attention to them? We'll answer these questions and several others as we frame the value proposition that social media offer to government today.

Part Two is an in-depth exploration of social media tools. What are the most common social media tools used in government today? How do you pick the right tool for your own needs? We cover the major tools in great detail, provide several examples of their current uses in government, and offer you our thoughts on the pros and cons of each tool set.

Part Three of the book focuses on the strategy and policy aspects of social media. Tools without strategy are destined for a short shelf life. How do you integrate social media into an overall communication strategy? How do you build a participatory audience for your social media plans? Who in your organization should be involved in strategy development? What are the key elements of a social media policy? And how do you define and manage your employees' use of social media? We cover all of these topics in detail to help you design a strategy that is powerful enough to age gracefully yet flexible enough to accommodate the rapid changes in social media technology and trends.

And finally, in Part Four, we cover the future of social media in government. What are the emergent tools that we believe will become commonplace in the future? The book wraps up with a summary and conclusions about where you can go next with social media.

When you are done, we hope that you will get out and perform your own social media experiments. Learn from peers. Share your results. Join the conversation, and give us feedback on your experiences. We're looking forward to hearing from you!

August 2012

—Ines Mergel
Syracuse, New York
—Bill Greeves
Raleigh, North Carolina

ACKNOWLEDGMENTS

We could not have created this guidebook without the creative peers, coworkers, and government "rock stars" who continue to integrate social media into the fabric of government operations. During our research we found valuable contacts and generous contributors who were willing to share their ideas, their suggestions, and their examples to help us formulate a field guide for those who are (either by assignment or desire) following in their pioneering footsteps.

We found these innovators at all levels of government. We discovered them in different pay grades, varied organizational cultures, and unique job roles. Yet they all had a common goal of citizen service and a firm belief that the dynamic power of social media was a crucial component of moving their agencies forward. We would like to thank the supportive, creative, and tireless social media champions in organizations such as MuniGov and GovLoop. Thank you for your wisdom. We hope we have appropriately captured and illustrated your thoughts and ideas as a guide to those who are just beginning their social media journey.

We would like to thank our champions at Jossey-Bass/Wiley who believed in our concept for the book and helped us mold our thoughts and ideas into a polished and useful finished product. We would especially like to thank Alison Hankey, Dani Scoville, Byron Schneider, Nina Kreiden, and Elspeth MacHattie. Your encouragement and guidance kept us on the straight and narrow as we moved through our first book-writing experience.

We would also like to recognize those who provided case studies of their own professional and organizational experiences with social media: Chris Moore, Pam Broviak, Stephanie Slater, Steve Ressler, and Dustin Haisler. Your words underscore the guidance offered in this book with real-world, relatable examples for our readers. We would also like to offer our gratitude to our diligent and insightful peer reviewers. You helped us formulate a guide that was approachable, practical, and engaging for our shared peer group.

And finally, we would like to thank you, the readers of this guidebook. As you learn more about social media, you will join us in the understanding that social media are about communication and conversation. We hope that once you find a way into the social media world for your organization, you will close the communication loop by sharing your ideas, suggestions, feedback, and constructive criticism with us so that we can all benefit.

THE AUTHORS

Ines Mergel is an assistant professor of public administration at the Maxwell School of Citizenship and Public Affairs and the School of Information Studies (iSchool) at Syracuse University. She was previously a postdoctoral research fellow at Harvard's Kennedy School of Government, Program on Networked Governance and the National Center for Digital Government. Mergel teaches in the master of public administration program at Maxwell, where her courses address Government 2.0, new media management in the public sector, networked governance, and public organizations and management. Her research interests focus on informal networks among public managers and managers' adoption and use of social media technologies in the public sector. In particular she studies how public managers search for, share, and reuse knowledge they need to fulfill the mission of their agencies.

A native of Germany, Mergel received BA and MBA degree equivalents in business economics from the University of Kassel, Germany. She received a doctor of business administration (DBA) degree in information management from the University of St. Gallen in Switzerland and spent six years as a pre- and post-doctoral Fellow at Harvard's Kennedy School of Government.

Mergel's work has been published in a number of journals, including the *Journal of Public Administration Research and Theory, American Review of Public Administration*, and *International Public Management Review*. Her ongoing thoughts on the use of social media applications in the public sector can be read on her blog and on Twitter. She can be contacted or followed at

Twitter	@InesMergel
Blog	http://inesmergel.wordpress.com
Web	http://faculty.maxwell.syr.edu/iamergel

Bill Greeves is the chief information officer for Wake County, North Carolina. In the fall of 2008, Greeves cofounded MuniGov 2.0—a coalition of governments focused on exploring the use and principles of Web 2.0 in an effort to improve citizen services and communication via technology. This organization continues to grow and gain international recognition and praise for demonstrated leadership in the area of government social media.

Greeves is also a frequent public speaker and a nationally recognized resource on the topics of government social media, collaboration, consolidation, and cloud computing. His work has appeared in several periodicals including *Public CIO, Government Technology, Emergency Management*, the General Services Administration's newsletters *Government by Collaboration* and *dotgovbuzz, Governing*, the Alliance for Innovation's *Ideas Quarterly Report, StateTech*, and *Kommune21. Government Technology* magazine included him in its Top 25 Doers, Dreamers and Drivers in Public Sector Innovation list in 2010.

Prior to Wake County, Greeves served as the director of information technology for Roanoke County, Virginia, and for Hampton, Virginia. He has been working in municipal government since 2000. In his spare time, he is a writer of fiction. He lives with his family in North Carolina. He can be contacted or followed at

Twitter	@bgreeves
Blog	www.billgreeves.com
E-mail	bill.greeves@gmail.com
Skype	bill.greeves

Social Media in the Public Sector
Field Guide

PART ONE

How Did We Get Here?

We can adjust much quicker if we can figure out how to have this two-way conversation and if we can look at the public as a resource. The public is putting out better situational awareness than many of our own agencies can.

—Craig Fugate, director, Federal Emergency Management Agency, February 2011[1]

In the first part of this book we explore the origins of social media and review the value proposition that social media offer to governments. We identify and discuss the characteristics of social media in general and particularly how these media differ from traditional media. We also address the properties that underscore the value of social media: mingling, collaboration, communication, and community. We close Part One with a review of the reasons why social media have risen to such prominence today.

What Are Social Media, and Why Should Government Pay Attention to Them?

On December 6, 2010, the Virginia State Police (VSP) issued an Amber Alert for twelve-year-old Roanoke County, Virginia, resident Britney Mae Smith, after police found her mother murdered in their home. Police believed that Britney was traveling in her mother's car and traveling with her mother's thirty-two-year-old boyfriend, Jeff Easley. After releasing the formal Amber Alert through traditional communication channels, the VSP public relations team also posted the alert on the agency's Facebook page, instantly publishing the information to its 24,000 fans. Along with the alert, the agency posted photos of Smith and Easley and a description of the vehicle.

During the next several days, Facebook users shared the information about the alert with their personal networks as investigators followed up on thousands of leads. Fortunately, Britney was returned home safely, and Colonel Steven Flaherty, superintendent of the VSP, credited social media with assisting the police in the case: "Social media certainly enabled law enforcement to reach beyond our borders, our normal footprint. Britney Smith's disappearance and her search started with an Amber Alert. This outreach quickly, very quickly, spread with the effective integration of social media, the traditional media, and the traditional Amber Alert emergency alert system."[1]

On January 12, 2011, Facebook announced that it would begin issuing Amber Alerts as an opt-in newsfeed notification for users, thanks to a partnership with the National Center for Missing & Exploited Children and the U.S. Justice Department.[2]

So what are social media? And why should government care? The fundamental component of all social media—or the next generation of the interactive Internet—is a cultural shift, enabled by social networking platforms that transform linear give-and-take communication into a collaborative discussion. Over the past several years the rise of social media and their associated tools and methods have driven a new information paradigm and a new form of collaborative engagement in the public sector that has dramatically affected the ways in which governments communicate, build relationships, conduct business, and send and receive news and information.[3] The use of social media is oftentimes referred to under the umbrella term *Web 2.0*, which describes applications that allow for online interaction, including online social networks, joint content creation, and content sharing.[4] And although the terms *Web 2.0* and *social media* are closely associated with Internet technologies, these technologies are simply means to an end.

By December of 2008, the Internet had surpassed newspapers as the public's resource for daily news.[5] The earliest social networks evolved with a specific audience in mind (for example, MySpace was devised for teens and the earliest version of Facebook was for college students). Today's social media networks, such as Facebook and LinkedIn, have evolved around communities and connections that people share and have become a common point of reference in our culture. Today, blogs, wikis, and media sharing sites, such as Flickr and YouTube, and even raw data mashups are competing with traditional media and information sites. These have become the new resources that citizens use to gather news and information or to connect with events and organizations they care about (consider, for example, the use of social media in the emergency response to the earthquakes and tsunami in Japan in 2011).[6]

Social media have proven their staying power in that they have become tightly integrated into our lives. Traditional media now rely on social media accounts of events, as they occur, to provide updated information.

Colleges and universities have begun incorporating social media tools and concepts into the core curricula of their classes, understanding that digital literacy is a requisite for the future workforce. People across the globe are turning to social media to join the conversations that are of interest to them.

Through social media, citizens connect to a global community, carry on conversations, share ideas and information, and collaborate on whatever project holds their interest, whether it be a simple photo album, a blog, a school campaign, or a political revolution—like those that erupted in the Middle East in early 2011.[7] Those revolutions showed us that citizens, engaging in social networks, can have a massive, historic impact on their government. If governments cannot be a part of the active dialogue, they can at least listen. Hearing citizen sentiments will help them to determine whether or not existing policies are successful or need to be changed in order to more accurately represent constituents' requests.[8]

So why do those in the public sector need to pay attention? Social media may have once been a small ripple in a big pond. But that ripple has evolved into a massive wave of acceptance and use in online communities, education, media, and the private sector. This wave is here, today. The time is at hand for governments to decide if they want to ride the wave on their own terms, or risk being knocked down by it as it passes over.

Government 2.0—the use of social media in the public sector—is not just a fad. Instead, it has become an international phenomenon, going far beyond the U.S. context. Government agencies across the globe and at all levels are learning to adapt these new principles and technologies into their respective missions and goals. If agencies are interested in maintaining a flow of information with constituents and providing usable services, they must take the time to understand what social media are and learn about the relevant tools and how they are being applied in government today. At that point agencies can make an informed decision about how and when and why they will choose to use or not to use social media to meet their organizational goals.

Social Media Versus Traditional Media

Understanding the way social media work within government is perhaps a study in differences—differences between the forms of communication governments have had in the past and the forms both governments and citizens have available to them today. We will call these previous forms collectively *traditional media*. Traditional media have, for hundreds of years, had a one-to-many approach to communication:

- One TV network to many viewers
- One news anchor or radio show producer to many listeners
- One reporter, one publisher to many readers
- One city hall website to many visitors
- One press release to all citizens (via the local newspaper)

News, information, and service delivery have been developed, packaged, and distributed in a broadcast fashion.

Even with the advent of the web and the ability for readers to comment on what media deliver, with or without a moderator, those commenting readers have still been on the outside of the story. Readers have been empowered to comment on a given topic, but that content has still been a "done deal." It has been a (usually) complete thought, designed, constructed, refined, and published for consumption without any prior input from a community of users.

Today most government websites still only allow citizens to leave a comment via an e-mail submission form. Rarely are the comments directly posted to an agency's website. Responses to individual inquiries submitted in this fashion are sometimes not feasible. It is therefore no surprise that citizens find other forums in which to publish their sentiments online and find support for their ideas—thereby garnering social support within the community. In order to maintain communication relevance, agencies must work to incorporate these new methods into their communication arsenal. Additionally, if governments do not offer forums for engagement, citizens will find alternative forums for voicing their opinions, particularly regarding contentious issues and decisions.

In 2010, Amtrak customers were stuck for hours on a train during rush hour, as a result of a large power outage in Washington, DC. While Amtrak officials worked to restore power, Amtrak's communications group focused on providing details of the incident to traditional news outlets, using traditional media methods, rather than focusing on providing details to the railroad's own passengers through Twitter or the Amtrak website. Amtrak responded to media inquiries by returning journalists' phone calls but did not directly reach out to the travelers waiting on the train. Amtrak's Twitter account was used to provide information three hours later, after power was already restored. Much earlier direct contact with the customers through social media tools would have helped stranded passengers, increased transparency and accountability, and provided a valuable customer service.[1]

Figure 2.1 shows how web content was and continues to be created for the first generation of government websites. There is usually one webmaster who serves as the gatekeeper between the content producer and the website. The content itself is relatively static and updated periodically (with the older content moved to an archive), and the audience consists of relatively anonymous websurfers. Agency contact channels consist of directions for isolated, one-on-one encounters, in the form of office hours, a street address, phone numbers, a contact form, or a general e-mail address.

Fast forward to the present, and the world has an entirely new approach to the way information is produced, consumed, reformed, and reproduced. Social media do not just alter the way in which organizations communicate information. They fundamentally abolish the major tenets of traditional media, one by one, to create more flexible platforms that challenge long-held norms and that open pathways for collaborative content production outside traditional interactions, including formal government-to-citizen interactions (for an overview see Michael Wesch's YouTube video *The Machine Is Us/ing Us*).[2] Citizens can now simply post their

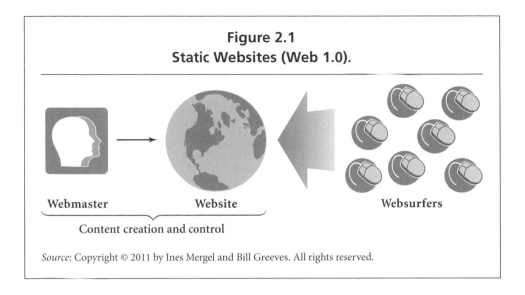

Figure 2.1
Static Websites (Web 1.0).

Webmaster   Website   Websurfers

Content creation and control

initial thoughts on a blog, Twitter, or YouTube. And then, if that initial thought engages an audience, a fan, follower, or citizen reads, thinks, and replies with a counterpoint, a disagreement, a validation, and so forth. Then perhaps a second reader also comments, providing yet a different point of view from that of the original author or the first reader. The original author or first reader, or both, may react accordingly and *voila*—conversation, community, and collaboration are born— snowballing pieces of information and sentiments throughout the whole social network of a community (or the world)! The writer becomes part of the story and becomes a reader as well. The readers speak their minds and wear the writer's hat with equal gusto. Intelligent government agencies pick up the trend and use the willingness of citizens to contribute. For example, the U.S. Geological Survey (USGS) tracks Twitter messages created by citizens regarding earthquakes felt in their neighborhoods and compiles this information on a Google map (Figure 2.2). Although the map won't be used as official scientific information, large numbers of messages create data points that can potentially produce insights for emergency responses—at a minimum the USGS is creating *citizen scientists* and demonstrating that government is listening to citizens and values their input.[3]

With Web 2.0, social media applications such as blogs and RSS feeds, accounts on social networking sites such as Facebook or Twitter, and joint content creation and sharing functions such as those offered by SlideShare or YouTube can be

Figure 2.2

Twitter Earthquake Detector (TED).

Department of the Interior
Recovery Investments   *Investing in America's Economic Recovery*

ABOUT   OVERSIGHT   BUREAUS   PLANS *and* REPORTS   CONTRACTS *and* GRANTS   CONTACT *us*

U.S. Geological Survey: Twitter Earthquake Detector (TED)

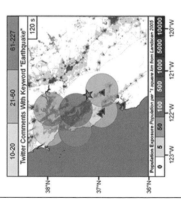

The U.S. Geological Survey is using funds from the American Recovery and Reinvestment Act to support a student who's investigating social internet technologies as a way to quickly gather information about recent earthquakes.

In this exploratory effort, the USGS is developing a system that gathers real–time, earthquake–related messages from the social networking site Twitter and applies place, time, and key word filtering to gather geo–located accounts of shaking. This approach provides rapid first–impression narratives and, potentially, photos from people at the hazard's location. The potential for earthquake detection in populated but sparsely seismicly–instrumented regions is also being investigated.

Source: U.S. Geological Survey, "Twitter Earthquake Detector (TED)," last updated February 2, 2012, http://recovery.doi.gov/press/us-geological-survey-twitter-earthquake-detector-ted2012www.doi.gov.

integrated into the traditional government website. The main authority for content creation is still in the hands of each website owner—the agency or department does not lose control over the formal message it is sending out. However, with social media the agency now has added additional layers of interaction. For example, a government agency could populate its Facebook page with content originally drawn from its official website in order to reach constituents who are active on social networks yet rarely choose to visit the organization's website directly. Government agencies can participate in or at least monitor issues being discussed within social networks, to ensure that they are more prepared when the issues are brought to them via a formal process. Moreover, government information can be put out in close to real time, allowing for fast dissemination that can be useful for quick polls, idea generation, and even responses to emergency situations. Citizens can repost, share, and forward content to their own networks, enabling government to reach larger audiences than before. Even though it seems as if government might be giving up control over its messages, it has at the same

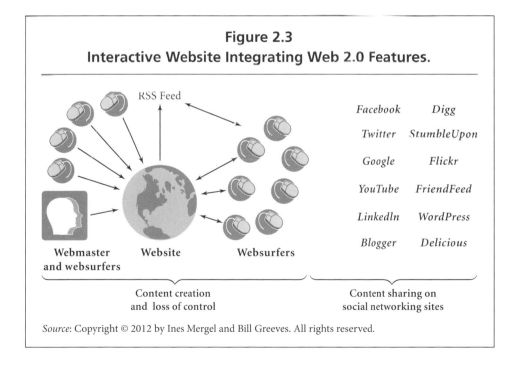

Figure 2.3
Interactive Website Integrating Web 2.0 Features.

RSS Feed

Facebook   Digg

Twitter   StumbleUpon

Google   Flickr

YouTube   FriendFeed

LinkedIn   WordPress

Blogger   Delicious

Webmaster   Website   Websurfers
and websurfers

Content creation   Content sharing on
and loss of control   social networking sites

time the opportunity to react much faster to rumors or to provide facts to counter conversations that have drifted in the wrong direction.

Figure 2.3 shows how social media channels are adding new outlets to the existing traditional information structure.

As Table 2.1 illustrates, social media differ drastically from traditional media. Roles, limitations, structure, and the general approach to the way information is communicated are experiencing a powerful reorganization. If government agencies can capture that reorganization and find ways to adopt it, or to adapt their current modes of communication to it, they can expect to make a successful transition to new channels and new audiences.

Table 2.1
Traditional Media Versus Social Media:
A Comparison of Characteristics.

CHARACTERISTIC	TRADITIONAL MEDIA	SOCIAL MEDIA
Responsibility for content	Usually a single author	Often shared
Content	Printed or produced and released	Subject to constant refinement
Delivery	One-way (sender and receiver are distinct)	Two-way (conversational, everyone is both producer and consumer)
Feedback mechanisms	"Letters to the editor" or static comments	Instant feedback and commenting capability (sometimes moderated)
Structure	Finite space and storage requirements and formats	No limitations on length or quantity
Prerequisites	Hardware, software, funding, corporate plan	Technology skills and Internet access
Permissions	Extensive copyrighting requirements, cumbersome sharing	Copyright issues still evolving, but easy sharing via linking

Transformative Properties

Throughout the history of democratic society, citizens have relied upon government as the sole authority for the provision of certain necessities in exchange for the payment of taxes. Government provides services (for example, trash collection, public safety, firefighting), information (such as how to start a business), and policy (such as building codes), all of which communities of citizens use or abide by. The citizens in turn are consumers of these necessities. Most government organizations find it imperative to provide the details of these products and services to their constituents in order to promote use and compliance and also to attain citizen buy-in and to ensure that the products and services remain on target.

Even though government units have become adept at providing information across many formats and channels, it is still basically a one-way communication stream. Take for example the mandatory interactions with government involved in the payment of taxes. Citizens submit their tax forms according to a well-publicized schedule, they pay amounts owed and perhaps fines, and the government issues any refunds due. Establishing additional, topical, two-way communication opportunities (for example, soliciting suggestions on improvements in the distribution of tax regulations in an open forum) can increase awareness and transparency and in turn, it may be hoped, increase trust and accountability in government.

Technology has of course drastically improved the reach and breadth of communication between citizens and government, particularly in the last few decades. Things like the World Wide Web, e-mail, emergency alert systems, and 311 phone centers have empowered governments to share more information and to do so in more formats simultaneously. This enables a government to provide better, faster services and information to larger audiences. Services are delivered as expected or else the citizens voice their demand for a change in direction via the democratic process of elections.[1] Social media provide citizens with highly interactive channels and fast exchange mechanisms for sharing feedback or complaints about the government, but oftentimes government is excluded from these social media processes and thus may miss the initial voicing of a demand for change.

But what about directing feedback so that government is involved and can proactively deal with the feedback? What about providing a voice to the citizens on the topics and issues that most affect them? How do governments harness the collective opinions and expertise of their constituents? And how do they extend their reach to gather valued input from all segments of the population, not just those who are heavily vested in the civic process?

The constraints of time and geography, or perhaps even a general apathy toward or ignorance of the workings of government, can make *citizen input* a labor-intensive proposition for both governments and their citizens. Governments offer in-person forums such as civic league meetings, city council meetings, and planning commission meetings to provide opportunities for citizen voices to be heard. They frequently issue surveys to gather data. They solicit opinions and have public hearings before an ordinance is passed. They offer phone numbers and e-mail addresses and website comment forms. But, regardless of the number of e-mails received or survey boxes checked, this process still is a linear, sequential flow of information, rather than a topic-focused conversation.[2]

How is a municipal government to be moved forward in the desired direction if it relies solely on a handful of survey responses or listens to the fifteen people who come to speak at a city council meeting? If those fifteen speakers are very unhappy about an issue, does that mean they represent the collective feelings of the other five, fifteen, or fifty thousand citizens? No, of course not. More likely it means that they were so irate about the issue that they took time out of their busy schedules to attend the meeting and voice their concerns. And of course that is a positive sign that the democratic process is working. However, the opinion of fifteen people is hardly a strong enough indicator of public opinion to direct a million-dollar decision or pass an ordinance that has community-wide implications.

So how do you expand that pool of participation? How do you collect input from those who may feel marginalized or are simply too busy to invest the time needed to attend a council meeting or other forum? How do you reach those who don't read the newspaper on a daily basis or watch television?[3] Traditional websites are not the answer either. Research shows us that most citizens do not rely on a government agency's website to find even such basic information as road conditions, answers to tax questions, or notices of community events.[4] Citizens tend to find the bureaucratic approach and sheer size of a government agency's website overwhelming and therefore do not visit a general government website to browse information or seek news. So relying on an online survey on your agency's own website is like putting a shining billboard on a backcountry road. It's pointless! You need to move the message and the debate to a forum where the people are. Enter Government 2.0.

The Social Media Ecosystem in the Public Sector

What is now called Government 2.0 has roots that stretch back several years. Many local and state government information technology (IT) professionals tried very early to find ways to integrate social media into their existing communication, collaboration, and community approaches. In 2007, the then chief technology officer of Washington, DC, Vivek Kundra, used a wiki to present requests for proposals in the acquisition process.[1] In 2008, as part of the Government 2.0 ecosystem, over 800 local government professionals found a way to share lessons learned and best practices in a virtual group, which they called MuniGov 2.0 (see www.munigov.org for information on how to join this group). At about the same time, GovLoop, the Facebook for government, was created, and by early 2012 it had about 40,000 users sharing information about Government 2.0–related topics.

Agencies and departments in the U.S. government have been using social media applications, such as Facebook pages, Twitter updates, YouTube videos, blogs, and RSS feeds, since 2009. This development was triggered largely by President Obama's memorandum titled "Transparency and Open Government," published one day after Obama's inauguration, on January 21, 2009. In this memo the president directed executive departments and agencies to increase open government in three distinct areas: participation, collaboration, and transparency.

President Obama's memo provides a mandate for the executive departments and agencies in the federal government. We have also observed a movement that is self-inspired, driven by the need for more transparency and community building, at the local and state government level.

Government 2.0 has quickly become synonymous with the use of the second generation of Internet technologies in government: highly interactive social networking services that allow real-time information sharing and bidirectional communication between citizens and between citizens and government.[2] The wide acceptance of social media tools provides positive proof that they are supporting the connection and networking needs of citizens. People frequently use Facebook to share success stories or report negative events in order to receive emotional support from their friends and family members. The direct and quick feedback circles on Facebook, created through *like* buttons or comments, provide a form of social justification that exists in the off-line world typically only through face-to-face interactions.[3] Social media establish global connectivity from the comfort and security of a personal device.

ESTABLISHING TERMS OF SERVICE PROVIDED GREATER ACCESSIBILITY

In the first year of the Government 2.0 movement, most federal government agencies were hesitant to dive into social media. At the federal level the transparency and open government memo was quickly followed by a series of necessary changes, such as the terms of service agreements (TOS) with social network services providers negotiated by the U.S. General Services Administration for government agency use,[4] the U.S. National Archives and Records Administration's social media record-keeping guidelines,[5] the Library of Congress's decision to archive all tweets;[6] and the changes made in 2010 in the cookie policy in order to allow government agencies to collect user data.[7] On a similar path of acceptance, the National Association of State Chief Information Officers (NASCIO) has also participated in successful negotiations with Facebook in order to modify terms of service. These negotiations have made social media requirements more palatable to the needs of local and state governments.

Figure 4.1
Library of Congress Announces
Acquisition of Twitter Archive.

Library of Congress
@librarycongress

🐦 Follow

Library to acquire ENTIRE Twitter archive -- ALL public tweets, ever, since March 2006! Details to follow.

50+
RETWEETS

50+
FAVORITES

11:36 AM - 14 Apr 10 via web · Embed this Tweet
↩ Reply ⇄ Retweet ★ Favorite

Source: Library of Congress, [Tweet announcing Twitter archive acquisition], April 14, 2010, http://twitter.com/#!/librarycongress/status/12169442690.

It was on April 14, 2010, that the Library of Congress announced that it had acquired the entire Twitter archive (Figure 4.1). This was a big step forward in reducing some of the hesitation social media directors, especially those in federal departments, were facing; up to that point, departments and agencies had not known how long they had to retain Twitter messages for public record-keeping purposes.

These new guidelines and modifications made the concept of social networking applications more appealing to government agencies. Today many agencies comfortably maintain a presence on Facebook, YouTube, or even Twitter in order to add new channels for the distribution of information. These new channels are in addition to the traditional information channels, such as the core website, TV ads, paper mailings, e-mail newsletters, and press releases. Given the rather disruptive nature of these new information channels and the innovation inherent in increased and direct citizen interaction, it is necessary to understand how and why agencies use these tools and what their potential impact might be.[8] Throughout this book, we will discuss a series of business cases and value propositions for the use of social media in government in much greater detail.

SHARING DATA, SHARING EFFORT

Today, in addition to a growing level of comfort with social media and two-way communication in formal agencies, a parallel movement is also observable on the citizen side. So-called civic hackers, citizen journalists, and citizen scientists, or what some might call *alpha geeks*, with a vested interest in government, are using social media tools with ease and are creating mashups using free and open source tools (such as wikis) to co-create content.

Consider the "collaboration" between the National Oceanic and Atmospheric Administration (NOAA) and the Weather Channel. NOAA produces national weather data and feeds them for free to specialty sites, such as the Weather Channel. Government, in cases like these, is providing data that are being used by the private sector: that is, private sector applications are being built on existing government services.

Another influential development is the Open311 movement—a collaborative effort to create open standards for 311 services. Open311 services connect 311 data collected by local governments with location-based data to create more effective public services (Figure 4.2). For example, CrimeReports.com works with data police departments collect and displays this information on maps (Figure 4.3).

The Government 2.0 movement therefore has produced not only government innovations but also innovations developed by crowdsourcing among citizens or civic hackers. Government 2.0 *Barcamps*, also known as *unconferences*, have helped to organize the movement and have also resulted in initiatives, such as CrisisCommons.org, and start-up opportunities, such as SeeClickFix—efforts designed to engage citizens in community issues.

These examples show that the Government 2.0 movement has developed itself from a "Wild West" of the use of open data and social media applications to an organized movement and even a convergence and consolidation with tangible outcomes, such as public services, with value for all citizens.

Figure 4.2
Open311.

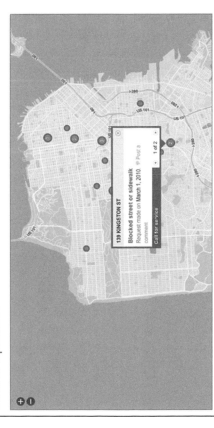

Source: Open311, "What Is Open311?" n.d., http://open311.org/learn. Used with the permission of Philip Ashlock.

Figure 4.3
CrimeReports Map.

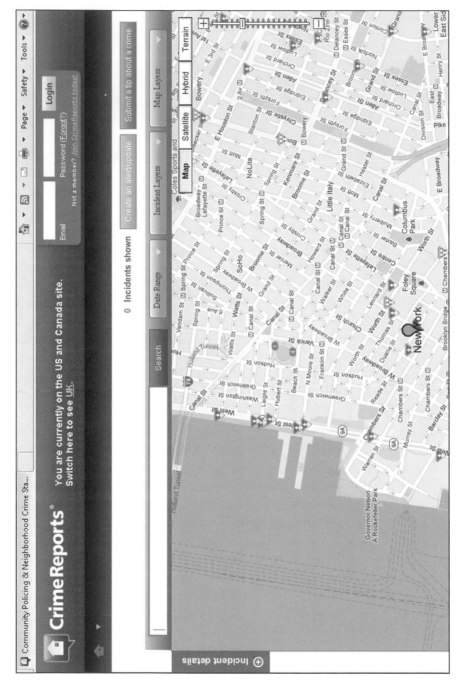

Source: CrimeReports, [New York City map showing crime reports], n.d., http://www.crimereports.com. Used with the permission of Public Engines, Inc.

Social Media in Action

The use of social media in government and, largely, Government 2.0 as a concept are focused on democratizing democracy—making it easier for a government to interact with its constituents in a productive environment of collaboration. Social media ask that (and perhaps demand that) governments accept a paradigm shift in the way they interact with stakeholders. Using Web 2.0 technologies moves governments beyond their traditional one-way release of services and information. It establishes a framework of collaboration in which stakeholders not only have the ability to become more easily informed about government decisions but also have at their disposal facilitated participation in such decisions.

Government 2.0 is not meant to replace more traditional methods of communication and service. Organizations can simply incorporate these new channels to deliver service in a more comprehensive format. Although Government 2.0 practices are not going to be the cure-all for all the issues facing a government organization, they bring substantial resources to the task of meeting the mission of citizen service. Later in this book, we will discuss specific technologies that have been applied in the Government 2.0 arena. But before we go further, it is important to understand that at its heart, Government 2.0 is *not* about technology. The truest value of Government 2.0 lies in its ability to guide an organization to transform its culture, adopt social media tools, and interact comprehensively with its diverse audiences.

Through our observations and our search for commonalities in social media implementations across governments and government agencies, we've identified four concepts that characterize Government 2.0 approaches: (a) mingling (rather than lecturing), (b) collaboration, (c) communication, and (d) community. These appear to be the consistent tenets that make for a successful deployment of social media in the public sector.

23

MINGLING

Think of the traditional government interaction as a lecture hall on a college campus. Primarily, the professor (that is, the government) does the "talking" (in the form of news releases, presentations at community meetings, and decisions made by legislative, executive, and judicial government bodies), and the students (citizens) listen, ask questions, take notes, and complete the homework assignments dictated by the professor. Yes, it works, to a degree. But this formula is stale and by its very nature does little to empower or enable the citizenry to communicate or vocalize concerns or ideas on a level playing field.

Government 2.0 transforms that lecture hall into a social event, with a government agency as the host. It's a more relaxed and casual atmosphere—think socialization, think building new relationships and identifying the threads of connectivity that link people. As the conversation continues, those ties grow stronger and more valuable to all attendees. But it takes time and effort to cultivate the relationships. As a host you must circulate, make introductions, refill drinks, provide finger foods, and so on. You *do not* walk into the room, pontificate, and then leave with the full expectation that people were impressed with you simply because *you* have spoken. You approach the topics and the scenario with an expectation of a give-and-take discussion.

Government 2.0 rests solidly on a foundation of *collaboration*, *communication*, and *community*. Take any one of these bases out and you do not have true Government 2.0. Instead, you have a hybrid approach that can move your organization forward, but not with the thoroughness and meaningful value you will get out of fully embracing Government 2.0.

COLLABORATION

Government 2.0 relies on the simple proposition that via collaboration we can create a better product than we ever could have completed on our own.

Break the static mold of serving up content to be consumed (documents to download, council meetings to watch, taxes to be paid) and complement this content with the tools that put people in touch with your organization on *their* terms. This connection can take many forms, and those forms are constantly evolving in response to consumer demand, bandwidth availability, and good old usability. Think of collaboration as your framework and your guiding principle moving forward.

The most innovative governments are now finding ways to use collaboration to crowdsource and gain insight from the collective knowledge of large groups of their constituents. For example, in 2009, the U.S. federal government launched Data.gov, a site that makes many kinds of government datasets available to the general public for use in new applications, mashups, and services that are enhancements to public services. The road map Data.gov is now following is leading this government website to connect with datasets from states, municipalities, and universities that can be the raw materials for even more service offerings.

Apps for Democracy is a competitive program that enables localities to engage their citizens in suggesting and building new technology applications and citizen services that make use of government-provided open data. The charter round of the competition, focused in the District of Columbia, cost taxpayers $50,000 and resulted in forty-seven web, iPhone, and Facebook applications, with an estimated value "in excess of $2,600,000."[1] (Figure 5.1 displays the original web page for this contest.) Using small cash investments and then taking the time to collaborate with constituents, localities are beginning to realize dramatic returns on these investments. Two recent federal competitions are the U.S. Environmental Protection Agency's Apps for the Environment (www.epa.gov/appsfortheenvironment) and the U.S. Department of Health and Human Services' Health Data Palooza (www.hhs.gov/open/discussion/2nd_annual_health_data_initiative.html).

COMMUNICATION

Communication is a bedraggled word in the public sector. Everyone agrees that communication is valuable, and it would be difficult to locate many who would admit to doing a lousy job at it. But the truth is, we *all* fail at it sometime. Central to effective communication is a solid understanding of your audience, aka your community. Too often agencies make assumptions about how people want to get information and interaction. Agencies risk a jump to a conclusion based on a personal frame of reference, and then compound the mistake by building grandiose information silos on structures that make little sense to a community.

So, how do you avoid that or, if necessary, fix it? Simple! Go out among the public, and take a stroll through what works for them. Web 2.0 didn't evolve as business tools; it evolved out of that stuff that turns people on—common interests, friendships, family videos, and the like. People became interested and familiar

Figure 5.1
Apps for Democracy.

with these tools because they *wanted* to, not because they *had* to. So the trick is to move beyond the traditional government space and get out to where the fun stuff is happening. A frequent mantra of many social media evangelists is "We need to be where the party is!" Learn to integrate messages, tools, and services into the media and forums that people are already accustomed to and use by choice. Communicate on their terms, using their tools and within their time frames.

COMMUNITY

The final tent pole of the Web 2.0 effort is *community*. Community is an essential part of creating a meaningful and valued government "of the people." Community is your audience. When you do not know your audience, your message and your methods might let you reach a small percentage of your desired audience but never the larger parts. As with communication, you find your community by evaluating and implementing the methodologies that are used by your audience. Post your news and information in the appropriate forums through the same methods your desired audience uses, and your community will find you.

You can develop your own following of people who have sought you out and found your information to be useful to them. And as that community evolves into considering new ideas and new innovations, it begins to sound very much like collaboration, doesn't it?

To be clear, we are not suggesting a three-ring, no-holds-barred circus act at your service counters. We are talking about taking an innovative yet measured approach to adopting the four principles discussed in this section. Many government organizations were leery of the Web 2.0 world at first glance, and rightfully so. As stewards of the public dollar, governments do not want to ever be accused of "goofing off on Facebook" on the taxpayer's dime. And all agencies have justified fears concerning security, privacy, legal data retention requirements, and ways to ensure that new services comply with regulations regarding public forums and records management. Sure there is work involved, but that is to be expected, particularly in the public sector.

If the members of your organization can have an honest, open-minded discussion about the directions in which communication and service delivery are evolving and how to keep up, we believe the naysayers and the fence-sitters will be willing to come together with the early adopters to solve those problems for the greater value that Government 2.0 brings to the organization.

CHRIS MOORE

CIO, City of Edmonton, Alberta, Canada
The Power of Social Media

I am not sure if I am an early or late adopter of social media, but one thing that I am certain of is the *power* of social media. I joined Facebook in 2006, mostly to keep track of what my two sons were doing in that space. I have been in the IT industry for over twenty-nine years, and I wanted them to embrace technology, not be afraid of it.

It wasn't until I joined Twitter in early 2009 that I understood the power of the human network. I have this basic theory that for the most part people want to be involved in a community. People live in cities with other like-minded people; they join clubs, have friends, go to work, and have families. When I joined Twitter, I discovered a whole new world, a whole new global community filled with like-minded people.

I have to admit, at first Twitter was difficult. A friend and colleague from Johannesburg, South Africa, @RoyBlumenthal, gave me some great early advice—*immerse* yourself. Decide that there are ten or so people that you will follow, read their every tweet, understand who they are and what they are thinking, do that for a month, and you will get Twitter. I took Roy's advice and I have never looked back. In the grand scheme of things I don't have many followers; however, in my mind it is not the number of followers that matters, it is the quality of the people. The people I follow and the people that follow me are a choice. That is the great thing about Twitter (and other social media tools)—it is an opt-in or opt-out world.

Since immersing myself in social media I have ventured far beyond the worlds of Facebook and Twitter. I also use LinkedIn, foursquare, Empire Avenue, Google+, Tumblr, Flickr, YouTube, Paper.li, and Tripit. I use these platforms for many different purposes and with some automation. When I use foursquare, a location-based social media platform, it updates my Twitter, which then updates my LinkedIn and Facebook accounts. The quickest way to see all of my social media activity is through my webpage, www.chrisj-moore.com.

So many people I talk to feel that they don't have time to spend on all these social media platforms. I encourage them to consider that it is not about time—it is about priorities. People who choose to make social media a priority are people who are building and growing relationships, often around the world. Social media have no boundaries and do not recognize time zones or socioeconomic classes. The power of social media removes barriers and creates new connections. All one has to do is look at the results of social media in relation to the Arab Spring of 2011 or the Occupy movement, both powered by people using social media.

As the chief information officer for the City of Edmonton, I find that social media have opened a whole new world of possibilities. As I mentioned previously, social media are incredibly powerful tools for building relationships. Through the use of my multiple accounts, I have been able to connect with other professionals, organizations, and governments that are interested in the work that we in Edmonton are doing. Without this technology it would have been difficult for us to connect in a meaningful way. In some circumstances all the work that we have done with some of our partners has been online. I have even had the opportunity to give presentations through a variety of digital platforms, including Twitter.

For an individual, social media are incredible tools. For organizations, they are even more powerful. Organizations that have matured in their use of social media have moved beyond seeing them as just another channel or as a way to reach youths; they are engaging with customers, citizens, employees, and partners. I recently blogged about the Fairmont Hotel in Victoria, British Columbia, which to my mind is a master at leveraging social media for customer service. (Check out the blog post at chrisjmoore.tumblr.com/post/10702400441/thx-fairmon tempress-a-star-amongst-the-fairmonthotels.) I have also had the honor of speaking to audiences around the world on the power of social media, in a presentation I call "10 Social Media Imperatives"—prezi .com/_nrcluxatgmq/chris-moore-10-social-media-imperatives.

One thing I encourage everyone to do is to join a social media network. In doing so, you are choosing to be part of the conversation and part of a community. Social media enter you into a powerful, world-wide, barrier-free conversation.

What's Driving Social Media Adoption—and Why Is All This Happening Now?

Technology continues to drive innovation forward and vice versa. But as we've already stated, social media are not about technology per se. Yet technology certainly has brought social media into being. So how did the evolution of technology and the cultural changes that technology brings lead to the use of social media in government? We have identified three drivers enabling citizens and government agencies to join social media–based discussions. These drivers are (a) the connectedness brought about by the growth of broadband and mobile devices and of online resources, (b) the changing expectations of the incoming workforce, and (c) the cost reductions and customer service value offered by social media tools.

CONNECTEDNESS

Technology has brought people together in unprecedented ways in the past decade. Networking giant Cisco predicts that the number of mobile-only Internet users will reach 788 million by 2015.[1] Over two-thirds of the adult population of the United States now has broadband Internet access at home. Seventy-nine percent of the country's adult population uses the Internet on a regular basis.[2]

In early 2012, there were over 800 million Facebook users worldwide. Twitter users were sending an average of 340 million tweets per day![3] A March 2011 study showed that teenagers who texted were sending an average of 3,276 text messages per month.[4]

When it comes to information, we all want it all and we want it now. Google enables *billions* of searches every day. Even though the Internet is not necessarily the best source of verified, accurate information, it is without question the most expedient way to get answers. Perhaps we even take for granted how wired we are and how easy it is to access information, services, and news online. When there is an outage of our favorite site or service, we are bothered and even indignant that we don't have the instant access and gratification to which we have become so accustomed. Many of us might even feel the physical pangs of withdrawal if we unexpectedly lose Internet access or cell phone coverage.

We are connected today in ways that were considered science fiction only a few decades ago. As the growth of smart and affordable mobile devices, online communities, and innovative technology platforms explodes across the planet, the barriers of time, geographical distance, and financial costs have been dramatically diminished. This shrinking planet and growing connectedness leads to new relationships, new resources, new communication methods, and the fresh collaborations that drive innovation. Governments now have cheaper, easier access to a wider pool of voices than ever before, a pool they can tap into to crowdsource ideas, visions, strategies, and the like, and to obtain qualified feedback, all of which can help them make the difficult decisions faced by the public sector.

EXPECTATIONS OF DIGITAL NATIVES

The makeup of government organizations is changing as older employees reach retirement age and agencies strive to hire the best and brightest from the available workforce. The members of the generation known as the Millennials (those born between 1980 and 2000, approximately) are entering the workforce today.[5] They are here, and they are not interested in the traditional worker bee ways of doing things. Newspaper ads and recruiting fairs are *not* going to cut it. The members of this new workforce generation grew up immersed in a digital environment. They are innately comfortable with consumer-focused technology. They expect to be in control of their own techno-destiny. Traditional office walls and eight-to-five working days are not signs of success but rather constraints. Millennials generally prefer a blurring of work and leisure and expect to have direct control over their work environment, their work tools, and their "content." They are not going to be drawn to a predetermined life in the government cube farm. They are not lazy or unmotivated, but they do have a radically different approach to performance measurement and productivity, one that many traditional government employees might not be used to or comfortable administering. Moreover, they represent the ever-growing number of citizens with similar attitudes and expectations of real-time responsiveness and feedback cycles in government.[6] That means, if governments do not actively work to engage on their terms *and* show them that there really is a pulse in the hallowed halls, government job openings are going to be passed over like those mediocre, store-bought cookies whose very presence taints the sanctity of the dessert table at office parties.[7]

If you want to find new talent that will put a fresh, friendly face on your organization, you've got to come to terms with this new approach to employment expectations and with 24/7 access attitudes. Governments that recognize this are beginning to incorporate social media skills into their job descriptions and job postings. In early 2011, New York City hired its first *chief digital officer* to assist the city to "develop forward-thinking policies on social media, digital communications, Web 2.0 initiatives, and other tools to better serve the public."[8]

Many in the Millennial age bracket are adept at using social media—both the tools and the concepts. Look around your organization today and spot those Millennials—they will be very useful later on when we talk about developing a workgroup to help you put your agency's social media tools into practice.

COST REDUCTIONS THROUGH MORE SOPHISTICATED SOCIAL MEDIA TOOLS

Even in the most stable and positive financial times, public sector agencies are under constant scrutiny when it comes to spending habits. It is imperative for them to find cost-effective ways to deliver those services they are chartered to provide. Social media tools are easy to learn and offer fast, simple, and affordable channels to "get the word out" and invite feedback. Tools such as Facebook have developed—with the assistance of massive criticism and feedback from their users—into sophisticated forms of networking that make it possible and acceptable for hundreds of millions of users to co-create content and share information with others, even those who are far outside each other's personal social circles. Setting up a Facebook page for a government agency is a relatively simple process (maintenance is another issue), and with just a few clicks city hall can reach citizens it was never in contact with before.

Summary Review

- Government 2.0—or the use of social media in the public sector—has become a worldwide phenomenon that governments need to treat seriously as a communication mechanism. Examples of the importance of social media to public life include not only the role of social media in the recent uprisings and revolutions in the Middle East but also, on a less dramatic but nonetheless critical plane, the ongoing technology-driven changes in citizen behavior that affect where people look for news or to discuss important issues.

- In contrast to traditional media, social media allow bidirectional interaction, reach larger audiences, and have users who co-create and share content, using Web 2.0 tools.

- As a result of developments resulting from the Open Government Initiative, a whole Government 2.0 ecosystem has evolved: government makes a sizable portion of the data it collects available through websites such as Data.gov; then civic hackers, journalists, and the public use these data to create applications.

- As described in Section Five, the main activities that social media promote are mingling, networking collaboration, bidirectional communication, and community building.

- The three main drivers for Government 2.0 development are connectedness, which results from technological advances and the maturing of social networking platforms; the expectations of the digital natives who are now entering the workforce; and the agency cost reductions and customer service increases made possible by social media tools.

PART TWO

The Tools: Where Do I Start?

> *There's no need to re-create everything from scratch....*
> *Look at some of the early adopters, see what they've done*
> *and see if it makes sense for your organization. And then*
> *think about what you need to do to customize it.*

—Dave Fletcher, Utah's Chief Technology Officer[1]
(Quoted with permission.)

The realm of social media contains hundreds of tools and services. How and where do you get started? There is no one true path to take, but there are specific groups of technologies that have already proven successful in many government organizations, particularly here in the United States. In the five sections of Part Two, we focus on social networking platforms, blogs, microblogs, and wikis because they are the most prominent social media tools in government. We also include real-life examples to inspire your efforts.

One important thing to remember about these tools is that you can use them as tools both for yourself as a government representative and for your organization as a whole. You may find great success in establishing a Twitter account for your locality, and then turn around and establish a social network account for yourself that is focused on peers in your role or in your field. After you've learned more about the pros, cons, and details of these popular tools, we encourage you to explore them further and to squeeze opportunity out of them both for yourself as an individual and for your organization!

Social Networking Services

There are literally hundreds of social networking services (SNS) available, most with similar features, such as profile pages for individual users and friending features for connecting with other members. SNS help users connect with other, selected network members—these *friends* lists are usually public or at least visible to all those connected by choice to each other. SNS enable members, who may be individuals or organizations, to post updates about their own statuses, link to other digital content, and thereby raise social awareness and prompt dialogue among members regarding their shared interests.

Networking platforms excel at being highly interactive and based around communities and groups. Commenting functions allow for *real-time feedback*. As an organization posts an update, *fans, followers,* or *friends* can immediately comment on the update, can use the *like* button to show support or interest, and can share the update on their newsfeed—thereby reaching potentially unlimited numbers of people in their own social networks.

Social networking services offer organized information designed to facilitate two-way communication and interactions among public audiences, typically via the web and mobile communication networks. Social networking services enable governments to present themselves *where the people are*. Social networking sites such as Facebook, LinkedIn, and MySpace offer gathering places where millions of people visit each day to keep up with the latest content shared by their friends and connections. It might be to gossip; it might be to job hunt or simply to pontificate. But people are there, in droves that continue to expand. SNS are therefore the places where constituencies pay attention to updates—whether they come from personal contacts or their local government. The purposes and functions of social networking services have evolved through user preferences and the responsive adaptations of the sites to their users over time. SNS are a powerful way to *reach an online audience*. Table 7.1 provides a brief overview of the best-known social networking services and the ways governments are using them.

Facebook is the best known of these networks. Over the past several years this service has seen tremendous growth. In early 2012, Facebook had over 800 million users across the globe, 25 percent of which were in the United States alone.[1] In March of 2011, the number of searches of Facebook's newsfeed surpassed searches performed on the Internet reference juggernaut Google for the first time.[2] This milestone marks a significant shift in the ways in people obtain information using the Internet. The reason for this shift is simple—we all tend to pay closer attention to those things our friends and trusted colleagues point to as being interesting, useful, or otherwise noteworthy. A link suggested by a personal connection automatically ranks higher in value than other links because it has been posted by a trusted source.

Facebook enables government individuals (such as mayors, city managers, police chiefs, and public information officers) and organizations (such as a public works department, a library system, a county, or a federal agency) to create an online profile that *complements traditional communication channels* with news, service information, opportunities, and requests for feedback in an online, accessible format. When your organization is on Facebook, other users are empowered to *like* your organization, which then enables you to share more media with them (photos, videos, web links, news releases, calendars, and the like).

In its early years, Facebook's primary user base was college students. Eventually, as these members graduated and became professionals, they took their social and alumni networks with them. Today the fastest-growing population segments on Facebook are professionals in the over-forty age brackets. They are, among other key citizen categories, current taxpayers, home owners, and parents with school-aged children.[3] These segments of Facebook's users may include constituencies who could offer your department or agency valuable feedback and input but who might not be able to come to regular town hall meetings. By using Facebook as a gathering point, government agencies have an opportunity to open a communication channel that can provide constant news and updates and can also combine that resource with real-time conversational opportunities in order to reach segments of the population that might otherwise be disinterested, disenchanted,

Table 7.1

Government Use of the Best-Known Social Networking Services.

SNS	DESCRIPTION	EFFECTIVENESS	GOVERNMENT USES	EXAMPLES
Facebook (founded 2004)	Originated as a social resource for college students; evolved into a broad social network with massive worldwide influence.	By far the most successful social network, Facebook is the primary social media destination for government organizations.	Virtual town halls, public education, public forums, community outreach, feedback solicitation, and so forth.	NASA's Facebook page: https://www.facebook.com/NASA.
Google+ (founded 2011)	Google's new online social networking platform, slowly picking up traffic.	Strongest new feature is Google+ Hangouts, offering video-supported, multiperson chats, including screen sharing; provides business and organization pages for government use.	Live interviews and chats.	Chicago Mayor's Office: https://plus.google.com/104762238087668104653; U.S. Marine Corps: https://plus.google.com/112094309462815325210.
GovLoop (founded 2008)	Specialized social network, sometimes called Facebook for government.	Holds strong interest for those in the public sector.	Peer networking, content sharing, job seeking, educational opportunities, and so forth.	Acquisition 2.0 (one of the hundreds of GovLoop discussion groups) examines the use of wikis to redesign the acquisition process at the GSA.
LinkedIn (founded 2003)	Social network designed for and focused on business users.	Of marginal interest for government agencies; targeted primarily at government employees as individuals.	Peer networking, job seeking.	Many topic-related discussion groups.
MySpace (founded 2003)	Early social network, geared primarily toward youths.	Rarely used by government organizations; popularity among target audience is waning, but it still has over 30 million users in the United States; content is focused primarily on pop culture.	Outreach, particularly targeted at young adults.	Brand pages.

or disengaged. The screenshot in Figure 7.1 shows a live town hall meeting on Facebook, with Facebook features that give audience members a way to chime in in ongoing conversations and to offer comments.

Government agencies rarely have the luxury of appealing to niche markets or captive audiences. Generally, by the nature of their mission, governments have to be all things to all people. This is especially true of municipal and state governments that are running dozens of quasi-independent service agencies. In carrying out their missions, many local and state agencies have found that a cohesive, self-service focused agency website can be a powerful tool, but it can also be a tremendous time and resource burden. If your organization does not have the funding, interest, or resources to maintain a dedicated website, social networking services can be an affordable and effective substitute. Although they may lack the integrated e-services commonly found on agency websites (such as bill payment or public works problem reporting), they excel in usability, content sharing, and bidirectional information sharing and dissemination. They also provide your citizens with the tools to self-organize around topics important in their communities.

Social networking sites such as Facebook enable their users to integrate other social media content (such as blog posts, RSS feeds, and YouTube videos) into their personal pages in order to offer information such as news, calendars, and the like. Thus a commonly used, heavily trafficked platform such as Facebook can easily provide the basics of content for a government organization. Facebook also offers a way to quickly poll your audience, with the *Questions* function.

THE DOWNSIDE

Even though social networks offer tremendous potential, there are a few drawbacks that you'll need to be prepared to address. Social networks, compared to other social media tools, can be complicated to fully utilize. Fully mastering widgets, features, and the integration of other social media tools into a social network can require time, patience, and a bit of technical skill.

Social networks can also be a visible target for derision within government organizations. Because so many individuals use Facebook, MySpace, and LinkedIn for personal reasons, some workplace cultures consider these SNS to

Figure 7.1

WhiteHouse.gov and Facebook Host Online Town Hall Meetings Live on Facebook.

Source: Facebook Live, [Town hall meeting with President Obama], 2011, https://www.facebook.com/WhiteHouse/app_3826979384208952.

be a time-wasting opportunity akin to online games. One government employee we spoke to gave us a poignant picture of the topic, recounting the stigma she felt after she had been assigned the task of establishing a social networking services presence for her agency: "I was constantly clicking the minimize button when coworkers walked behind me so they didn't think I was always goofing off, especially during the initial setup phase. Even though I'm the webmaster for the department, I was still afraid of coworkers gossiping—'Geez, she's always on Facebook. She never does any work'—when in reality I was working. It's often hard for others to accept that what you're doing on Facebook may be work related because what they're doing [on Facebook] is not."

KEEPING THE CONVERSATION GOING

Once you master a social media tool set and build a powerful network presence, you also have to develop an audience in order for the tool to be effective. Content, services, and information posted on a social network are valuable to the extent they are shared. Followers, fans, friends, and *likes* are crucial to squeezing value out of social networks. Trust is an essential component in building a willing and participatory audience. Posting timely, accurate, and useful content is a good way to start. Responding helpfully to comments (yes, even the negative ones!) is the best way to establish credibility (Figure 7.2).

If casual observers can easily see that you are engaged with and committed to your social network audience, you will be able to capture their interest, earn their trust, and facilitate their input on larger issues. In Section Twelve, we'll cover more ideas for building your audience.

In addition to being a cornerstone communication vehicle for your agency, a social networking service can also be useful for you as an individual, as a way to connect with peers and find resources relative to your position in the organization. There are many informal social networks exclusive to government. These informal, personal social networks offer shared spaces where government workers in similar roles or facing similar tasks can share discussions and best practices, vent to sympathetic peer groups, or even find new government employment. These informal networks are focused on their users as individuals, and so the level of etiquette, participation, and value will vary greatly from group to group and network to network.

Figure 7.2

Charlotte, NC, Fire Department Provides General and Proactive Information and Follows Up on Specific Inquiries in a Friendly, Effective Manner.

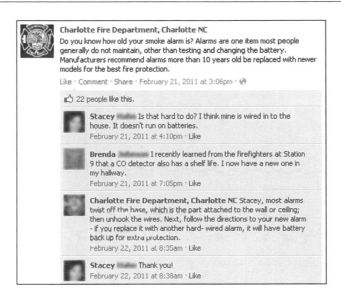

Source: Charlotte Fire Department, [Smoke alarm information], n.d., https://www.facebook.com/CharlotteFireDept. Used with the permission of the Charlotte Fire Department, Charlotte, North Carolina.

LinkedIn, casually termed *Facebook for professionals*, allows you to publish a formal presence focused on your résumé, professional interests, and connections with colleagues. GovLoop.com, the *Facebook for government*, is another powerful resource for government employees. Originally established as a side project by a federal government employee, the site has grown to over 40,000 members within two years and has become extremely popular among government employees for sharing insights, looking for feedback, and discussing ongoing issues and projects (Figure 7.3). In the following case example, GovLoop founder Steve Ressler describes the history and purpose of this resource.

In Part Three, we will talk more about *acceptable use* of social networking services and the blurring of professional use and personal use in government agencies.

Figure 7.3
GovLoop Is an Open Social Networking Platform Designed Exclusively by and for Government Employees.

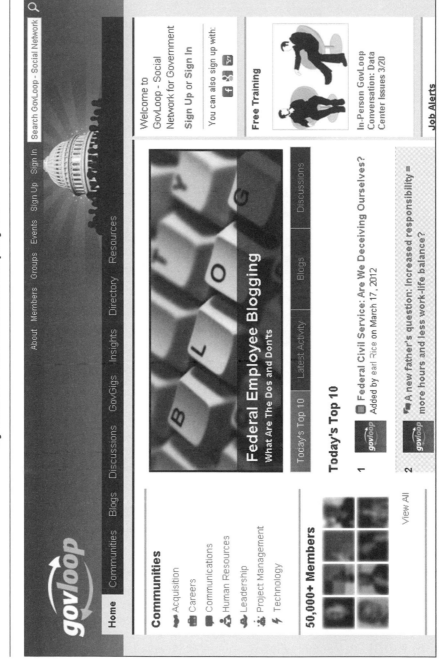

Source: GovLoop, [Welcome page], n.d., http://www.govloop.com.

HOW DO WE SOLVE THE KNOWLEDGE GAP IN GOVERNMENT? THE GOVLOOP STORY

Steve Ressler

Founder and CEO, GovLoop.com

Times are tough in government. Budgets continue to be shrunk and agencies are being asked to do more with less. The workforce is changing as the baby boomers are beginning to retire, plus agencies are pushing furloughs and layoffs. At the same time, citizen demands are rapidly changing as technology continues to change at rapid speeds in our consumer lives.

So what can government do?

To me, it should begin by leveraging its collective brainpower.

The beauty of government is we are all on the same team. This is not Red Sox versus Yankees, Apple versus Google. City of Cincinnati is not a competitor to City of Los Angeles. Environmental Protection Agency should be learning and sharing resources with Centers for Disease Control.

I started GovLoop.com based on a simple experience as a government employee. Each day, my boss would ask me to do simple tasks—look into implementing a new technology, create a statement of work for a new contract, or launch a new recruitment program.

And each time I thought to myself—I bet someone else in government has already done this. Why am I re-creating the wheel?

So in June 2008, I launched GovLoop.com, a social network for federal, state, and local government leaders, to solve this problem. At its core, it is a site to help you solve your problems at work—find another government leader working on the same problem, ask the question you are facing, or read a blog post on a related topic. Three years later, our community is over 50,000 members strong, ranging from topics like project management to social media to acquisition. Each month, there are thousands of blogs and discussions where people are solving real problems and learning how to do their job better.

Just today, as I write this, a local government IT leader just asked and received three examples of policies on dealing with participating in software beta programs. Three discussions down, a discussion on the relaunched USAJOBS website (flagship job site for government) has over ninety-two ideas on how to make the product better . . . [ideas that were] synthesized and presented to OPM leadership.

In three years, our approach continues to evolve and together with our members we've launched free peer-to-peer mentorship, held over fifty free trainings where our members teach our other members on key topics from cloud computing to acquisition, and leveraged our crowdsourced approach to help senior leaders make better decisions. The best part of social media is that it changes every day and as a leader it is your responsibility to test, analyze, iterate, and evolve to truly focus on meeting the needs of your users.

In the end, social media should be looked at as an approach and tools to solve key problems whether that is citizen engagement or better customer service. The problem I'm passionate about is cross-government knowledge sharing and increased government performance.

Government has a huge knowledge gap as most agencies work in silos combined with little investment in internal knowledge management. When we add in the pending retirement tsunami, I think we are looking at an overall knowledge crisis which greatly impeded government performance.

I hope GovLoop can be a key part of the solution to the problem.

Social Networking Services Quick Start Guide

- Social networking services are built around communities and groups. SNS will allow you to establish connections, share online content, and enable real-time feedback. Remember that these networks are designed to facilitate two-way communication.

- There are several social networking services available, with Facebook being the most commonly used both in government and in the general population. Explore your options, and review the implementations of other agencies before selecting your path.

- Social networking services must be understood and adopted culturally within an organization in order to be effective. Be sure to provide the details and purpose of engagement with an SNS to your agency before you implement.

- Remember to post content frequently and keep up with comments and feedback in order to establish a positive reputation.

- Social networking services are valuable both to government agencies (for outreach and two-way communication) and to government employees as individuals (for peer communication, resource sharing, and job seeking).

Blogs

Blogs are online journals that typically contain reflections, opinions, and comments from one or more authors, and often hyperlinks provided by writers as well. Although blogs, short for *web logs*, have been around since the late 1990s (as *LiveJournal* and *Open Diary* have, for example), it has only been in recent years that governments have begun to employ them to share information and seek input.

For governments, blogs are an opportunity to put a fresh, friendly face on the business of government. Blogs tend to be personable, accessible in language and scope, and written in a casual, conversational tone. They provide an approachable message delivery system, even if that system is used simply to introduce readers to new concepts or projects or to summarize the current activities of an organization. The Portland Water Bureau, for example, injects its blog with science, news, and even humor to shed light on the complicated operations and projects required to maintain the city's valuable hydro-infrastructure (Figure 8.1).

Blogs serve as an ideal counterpart to what are often voluminous government websites. They allow an organization to summarize, highlight, and tie together online resources to provide a point of view or a progress report or to explain a decision or solicit feedback. They enable quick and sometimes informal updates and news blips on a given topic or project. Consider them as the social media version of a cover letter to a lengthy report or a progress report on a major initiative. The Centers for Disease Control and Prevention (CDC), for example, has used humor and creativity to underscore the value of preparedness. *Preparedness 101: Zombie Apocalypse* is a blog that communicates the essential components of an emergency preparedness kit and the value of an emergency plan in a fun and innovative way (Figure 8.2).

49

Figure 8.1
The Water Blog of the Portland Water Bureau.

POL → Government → Bureaus & Offices → Water Bureau → **Water Blog**

Recent Blog Posts | Water Service Insurance Offers: Read the Fine Print

Summer Supply Planning - Yes, already! - Printable Version - February 29, 2012 - 0 Comments

While summer may seem far away during this cold dreary season, our staff are already planning for the summer ahead, as well as learning from past summers.

Simply put, our winter rainfall determines our summer water supply. However, it gets very complicated when you add in factors like long term weather predictions, past and projected water demands, successful regional water conservation, native fish protection...and on and on.

To learn more about our efforts to consistently manage water supply in every season, visit our Seasonal Supply Planning webpage. Specifically, the "retrospective" provides details about the 2011 drawdown.

David Shaff
Administrator

Let's say for example that a city council approves a contentious measure to tear down a building in an historic downtown area and build a new library in its place. The debate and the decision have raised significant community interest on both the pro and con sides, and so all eyes are on the process—those in favor are eager to see the new facility open and those opposed are "watchdogging" to make sure the facility is in line with the charm and building standards of the historic district. In an effort to be transparent and inclusive, the city will want to post building plans, drawings, and project timelines on its website. It will hold community events to gather feedback on the library's features and services, and it will want to post these notices, meeting agendas, and minutes on its website. Perhaps it will install a public webcam so citizens can log in and view the progress. It will post bid solicitations for the jobs needed to get the project done. The amount of content and documentation relevant to this project will grow much more rapidly than the construction itself. By establishing a blog, written by the city manager's office or the public information officer, the city can provide recurring, accessible updates that summarize the latest project details and upcoming points of interest. It can provide a chronological journaling of progress in a summary format and can also offer insights into the process in a more informal manner than an official news release can.

In addition to providing various kinds of content, blogs should always enable *commenting* and *threaded discussion*. This is perhaps one of the most intimidating aspects of blogging in the public sector. In Part Three we'll discuss how to deal with inappropriate or off-topic comments in general, but agencies must be prepared to receive and respond to legitimate negative criticism. Most of the major decisions made in the public sector will draw fire from some constituency areas. This is to be expected; yet with blogs, agencies are providing critics with a way to raise those complaints and criticisms in a public, agency-sponsored forum. "Why would I want to bring that upon myself?" you might ask. The answer is that if you do not provide a forum, the vocal constituencies will find another channel that they will use to vent their opinions and to gain support for their particular points of view. A blog can help to channel comments and can act as a central communication platform where citizens discuss issues with each other—a platform in which you can participate. Establishing an open discussion forum will draw audience participation. You can retain this audience by enabling and encouraging feedback and comments. Respond in a timely, honest, and appropriate manner to these comments to maintain the necessary level of trust and interaction with your audience.

At the same time, it is important to have a comment policy. The *Ventura City Manager Blog* (Figure 8.3), for example, states a thoroughgoing comment policy that encourages dialogue yet establishes ground rules for all users:

By providing an open, online discussion forum, you can also proactively explain the basis and rationale for decisions. With each criticism or complaint

The goal of this blog is to provide a civic forum for real time news and dialogue regarding the City of Ventura. Comments are welcomed and encouraged. Here's our policy:

1. Stay on topic. Comments should relate to the topic being discussed in the original post.
2. Keep it clean. Comments should not contain profanity, racial slurs or any other derogatory terms.
3. Don't make it personal. Comments should not contain personal or defamatory attacks.
4. You don't have to agree with me. Reasonable arguments for opposing views are encouraged.

5. I don't have to agree with you. A posted comment is the opinion of the poster only.

6. All comments must be identified by the name of the person making them.

7. No campaigning. This blog is not the place to endorse candidates or a particular stance on a currently active ballot measure.

8. This comment policy may be revised at any time.

9. We reserve the right to prohibit comment submissions from individuals who repeatedly submit comments that violate this policy.

10. Your submission of a comment constitutes your acceptance of this comment policy.

you address via the blog, you are *enriching the value of the debate*. This does not necessarily mean that you will convince critics of the value of a particular decision, but it does solidify your commitment to open discussion. The blog also provides a *record of your explanation, rationale, or justification* in a nonconfrontational format, which may serve to open future doors to dialogue in the community.

Blogs require constant care and feeding if they are going to be recognized and viable outlets for communication. Draw in readers and participants by creating dynamic, relevant, and helpful messages on a regular, recurring basis. Consider establishing a publishing schedule to ensure that content stays fresh. The schedule should be realistically achievable (particularly if it is advertised), but do not let the blog go dormant. Regular updates ensure repeat traffic and new visitors alike. Be prepared to cordon off the time it takes to maintain the blog, and work it into a daily schedule.

Dave Ruller, city manager for Kent, Michigan, maintains a prolific and dynamic blog (Figure 8.4), often posting brief updates several times in a single week. Recent topics included the value of hydrant flushing, recognition of National Police Week, and a preview of summer construction projects throughout the city.

Figure 8.3
The *Ventura City Manager Blog*.

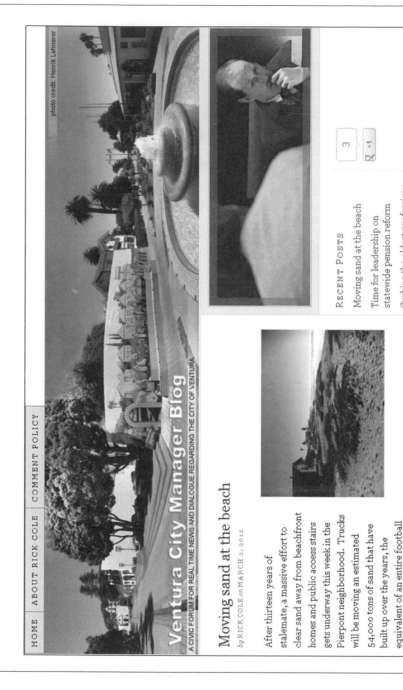

HOME | ABOUT RICK COLE | COMMENT POLICY

Ventura City Manager Blog
A CIVIC FORUM FOR REAL TIME NEWS AND DIALOGUE REGARDING THE CITY OF VENTURA

photo credit: Henrik Lehnerer

Moving sand at the beach
by RICK COLE on MARCH 2, 2012

After thirteen years of stalemate, a massive effort to clear sand away from beachfront homes and public access stairs gets underway this week in the Pierpont neighborhood. Trucks will be moving an estimated 54,000 tons of sand that have built up over the years, the equivalent of an entire football

RECENT POSTS

Moving sand at the beach

Time for leadership on statewide pension reform

Curbing the oldest profession:

3

Source: City of Ventura, California, *Ventura City Manager Blog*, March 2, 2012, http://cmblog.cityofventura.net/?q=cmblog. Used with the permission of Rick Cole.

Figure 8.4
The Kent City Manager's Blog.

Home | Kent City Management» | Economic Development» | City Services» | City Projects» | Citizen Info»

search

Many Voices, One Kent

Dave Ruller, Kent City Manager

City Dollars and Sense | City Living» | City University Stuff | General» | Services News | Taking Care of Business

Food Drive...

Posted by daver in City University Stuff on March 14, 2012 | No Comments

One of the best parts of living in a college town is being able to see the good things that students do in their adopted community.

The after-hours parties get more headlines but that's too bad because it only reflects a small portion of the student body and how they spend their time.

As City Manager I have had a chance to meet a lot of student leaders, and the administrators at Kent State University, that help channel all that positive student energy into projects throughout the Kent community – and Kent is a better place because of them.

Kent has a lot of great things going on downtown that hold promise for an economic recovery and a brighter future for all of us, but it's also a place that works hard to open doors to people from all socio-economic levels, making room for low income and distressed families that other communities have squeezed out.

Kent residents are proud of their socially conscious community but let's be frank, it

Social Kent 360

Source: Kent360.com, [City manager's blog], May 18, 2011, http://www.kent360.com. Used with the permission of City of Kent, Michigan.

Fortunately, blogs are forums in which it is easy to share authorship, which can assist with their critical, timely maintenance. An agency can delegate the responsibility for blog content to multiple authors, based on a division of topics or a simple rotation schedule. Enabling several voices to be heard around a core theme or blog focus enriches and diversifies the discussion, provides multiple points of view, reduces the time burden on individual authors, and improves accessibility and openness between your agency and your audience. Credibility and authenticity improve when you let your knowledge experts speak in their own voices—instead of responding only from a public affairs perspective.

Greenversations, the official blog of the U.S. Environmental Protection Agency, churns out frequent and diverse posts by sharing authorship among educators, scientists, enforcement agents, and other personnel. This blog also employs recurring themes, such as Science Wednesdays, to ensure a regular publishing schedule of relevant yet varied content (Figure 8.5).

Blogs can be hosted internally or externally through dozens of free, popular blogging platforms, such as WordPress or Blogger. By using tools such as Really Simple Syndication (RSS) feeds, content from blogs can be automatically posted to other social media outlets, including microblogs and social networking services, for additional exposure and cross-marketing of content. In addition, audience members can subscribe to an RSS feed using an aggregator, such as Google Reader or Yahoo Reader, and be automatically informed as soon as a new posting is added to the blog.

Blog Quick Start Guide

- Use blogs to summarize and or encapsulate large issues in a casual, approachable format. Blogs can be used to tie content and resources from disparate sources together in a cohesive, easily accessible format.

- Blogs are only effective when they allow (and preferably encourage) commenting and discussion. When your blog receives comments, be sure to answer them in a timely and appropriate fashion. Be prepared for legitimate criticism!

- Avoid apathy and stagnation. Post on a regular or frequent basis, and consider establishing a publication schedule.

Figure 8.5
A Science Wednesday Post on *Greenversations*.

Source: U.S. Environmental Protection Agency, *Greenversations*, May 18, 2011, http://blog.epa.gov/blog.

- Share authorship to prevent blog upkeep from becoming a time drain on a single individual or office in your organization.
- Use RSS feeds or other tools to post content automatically from blogs to other social media outlets, including microblogging and social networking accounts, in order to reach a larger audience without additional work.

Microblogging

Microblogging is a form of blogging that allows users to write brief text updates (usually with a maximum of 140 characters). The most popular of these services today is Twitter. The brevity of microblog posts creates distinct opportunities and drawbacks, different from those of a full-fledged blog. For government agencies, *tweets* sent via Twitter might consist simply of references to other online resources that are focused on an agency's news, events, or other public information, and thus might act to pull audiences back to, for example, the agency's website.

In the past three years Twitter has grown significantly, to over 140 million unique visitors in the United States in 2012.[1] News organizations, corporations, and recently also government agencies have picked up on this trend. Many government agencies maintain at least one Twitter account—some even manage multiple accounts, based on their operational needs and their diverse audiences. Oftentimes some agencies use their Twitter newsfeed as a *parallel publishing stream*—repurposing existing formal announcements, such as press releases, in order to push them out through this additional channel (we will discuss such social media tactics and strategies in Part Three).

Similar to blogs, microblogging services can be used to *distribute mission-relevant information*. Beyond the distribution of information also posted on blogs or on an agency's website, microblogs have the additional advantage of reaching followers with an immediacy that encourages them to forward these brief posts to others, ultimately creating snowball effects and allowing the agency to reach potentially unlimited numbers of people.

Snowballing exchanges of Twitter updates, aka tweets, can be described as public conversations, and they are not only improving transparency and accountability but also, when used appropriately, increasing the inclusion of public opinions into policy formulation, through information aggregation processes. Twitter can be used effectively to engage large numbers of citizens and create public conversations with this engaged, networked public. The outcome of these conversations can be new insights and even innovations in the public sector, suggestions on how to make government more effective, or simply repostings of vital emergency information in areas beyond the direct reach of government.

As Lee Rainie, director of the Pew Research Center's Internet & American Life Project, says, "The common reputation of Twitter is that it's frivolous, which isn't the case. If it's set up right, it's a rich environment of lots of learning and sharing of important material. It's not just 'what I had for breakfast.'"[2] Remember, it is isn't about new content or services but rather taking advantage of the new delivery methods. Twitter is very easy to set up and maintain. As a service Twitter can be compared to the short text messaging services on mobile phones, and tweets can arrive through a web interface or a text-enabled phone. One early noteworthy use of Twitter by government has been to send updates when fires are occurring to either inform the public in real time or to collect feedback from the public about the locations and extent of the damage. Figure 9.1, for example, displays a sample of tweets sent by the Los Angeles Fire Department (LAFD) giving near real-time dispatch information.[3]

In these days of shrinking travel budgets, Twitter users have also found that the service is useful as a back channel during presentations at conferences, to follow ongoing conversations that can help to bridge geographical distances. Other uses include simple informational updates, such as summaries of the prime minister's daily activities and priorities in the United Kingdom (twitter .com/DowningStreet), a Twitter feed with general countywide information in San Diego County (twitter.com/SanDiegoCounty), and a Twitter feed with prolific information on new titles, upcoming events, and so forth from the Roanoke County Public Library (twitter.com/RoCoPubLib; also see Figure 9.2). Government updates might also offer advice for marketing and tourism, economic development information, traffic advisories, updates on infrastructure or construction issues, and complaint reporting that can be combined with ongoing campaigns.

Figure 9.1
LAFD Twitter Updates and Alerts.

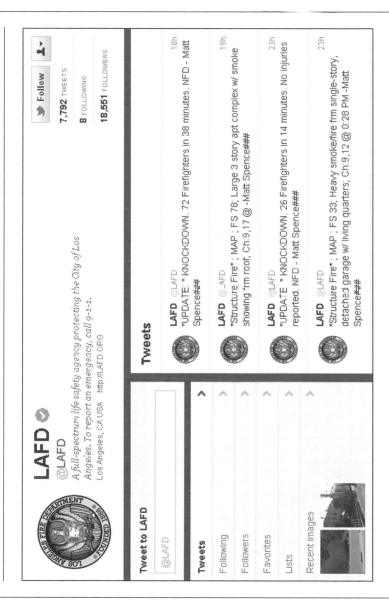

Source: Los Angeles Fire Department, [Twitter account page], http://twitter.com/LAFD.

Figure 9.2
Roanoke County Public Library Updates on Twitter.

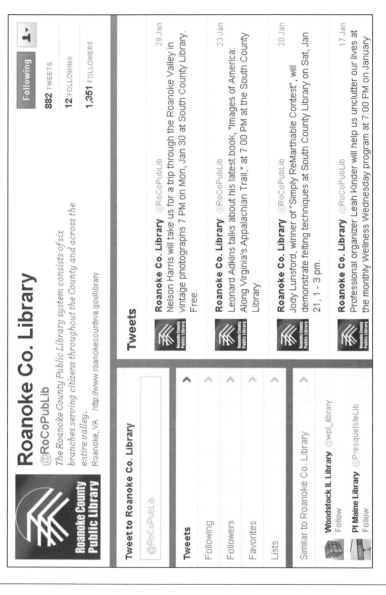

Source: Roanoke County Public Library, [Twitter account Page], n.d., http://twitter.com/RoCoPubLib. Used with the permission of Roanoke County Public Library, Roanoke, Virginia.

With the recent advent of the so-called social media revolutions in North Africa and the Middle East, many senior-level managers have started to pay attention to Twitter in order not only to understand how citizens are using it as an organizing tool but also to use it themselves as a tool for gauging the "temperature" among groups of citizens.[4]

A STEP-BY-STEP GUIDE FOR TWITTER ADMINISTRATORS

One of the big differences between Twitter and a social networking service, such as Facebook, is that Twitter employs an *asymmetric follower model*: anyone can follow a public Twitter account, without approval or expectations of reciprocity. (Twitter does offer the ability to protect an account by setting it up so that each follower must be approved by the account owner before content is viewable.) Also, as a government entity, your agency does not need to follow every one of its followers in return. This may lead to an imbalance in numbers, but there is no expectation of reciprocity. For example, the White House Twitter account currently has 2,102,602 followers but follows only 120 Twitter accounts. As you establish your Twitter presence, consider the content you want to deliver and the image you want to portray. Many government agencies tend to follow other government agencies at the local, state, and federal level. If you find other established accounts that help you achieve your communication goals, you may want to follow them as well.

You may also want to consider how you will handle the forwarding or sharing of someone else's message, known as *retweeting*. In other words, when a Twitter account holder finds your updates interesting and shares the original message with all of her followers, she retweets your tweet. Messages that are retweeted are highlighted with the RT symbol and with the name of the account that has retweeted the message. Retweeting is an easy way to reuse existing information that has popped up in your Twitter newsfeed. The web interface of Twitter.com currently does not allow any changes to the original message. Twitter desktop applications, such as TweetDeck, do allow editing so that you can enter your own content into the original message. Other practices include adding **H/T** or **HT** and the Twitter account where a specific message originated. This means that you are attributing content to another author—giving the recipient a *head tip* that you **Heard Through**, or heard the content elsewhere. Another practice is to add **OH** for **OverHeard**, to designate things you are sharing that you heard off-line (or at least not on Twitter). **OH** is usually used when no direct attribution to a specific Twitter user or other real-life person is possible or when you want to avoid embarrassing the originator of a statement. We recommend that government organizations always supply direct attribution and, as often as they can, reference the original sources for Twitter updates.

In cases where you would like to reply directly to a tweet from one of the Twitter accounts you are following, use **@replies**. Start your tweet with **@username**. The tweet will show up in your own updates and your followers can read it, but it will also show up in the newsfeed of the person to whom you are addressing it. The whole conversation—including retweets and **@replies** to the original message—can be traced by anyone who is interested in the *thread* (Figure 9.3).

Using **@replies** is also a good way to draw attention to a specific issue. For example, you might tweet about a town hall meeting, provide the URL to the meeting website, and add several organizational Twitter accounts (such as neighboring localities, local media, civic leagues, and so forth). The message then shows up in the accounts' newsfeeds and **@mentions** and likely increases awareness about the event or a piece of information you would like to share with them. Not only is this a way to increase social awareness but it also increases the likelihood that account holders will be willing to share the tweet with their own network of followers. Using **@mentions** also provides you with the opportunity to send a message to people who are not directly following you (see Figure 9.4). Instead of sending a direct message (through Twitter's messaging service), just use **@TheirAccountName** to send them the information or use **@TheirAccountName** to ask them to follow you, so that you can exchange direct messages with them.

The Twitter community has developed the practice of using the # sign as a *hashtag*. When it is placed before a specific word in a tweet, the resulting string can then be used as a search term to find all updates in the Twitter universe that also contain that term. Hashtags are a great way to categorize your updates and cater them to different audiences (Figure 9.5). The advantage is that you don't need to follow everyone who is using a particular hashtag; instead you can save a search for a specific hashtag (for example, **#gov20** for Government 2.0 or **#opengov** for open government) and go back to this search now and then to see what people are talking about. A hashtag is clickable, like a link, and it

Figure 9.3
Twitter Conversation About the Use of USGS Data to Provide Facts Used in a Movie.

Source: Scott Horvath, [Twitter account page], January 27, 2012, https://twitter.com/S_Horv/status/162914637824798720.

brings you directly to a list of all updates that have ever used the same hashtag. Very popular hashtags can become trending topics. Another Twitter tradition is **#FF**, which is short for **#Follow Friday** and which is used to start a message that points you to someone's favorite Twitter users. A **#Follow Friday** update includes a list of Twitter handles (**@YourName**) (Figure 9.6). Together with retweets, **#FF** marks what some people refer to as *Twitter love*—pointing your network to your favorite updaters will likely result in more followers.

Every day several hundred Twitter updates can pile up in your newsfeed, which can be discouraging and at times overwhelming. To avoid this, you can

Figure 9.4
An EPA Tweet Including @mentions and Hashtag.

Join @EPAwater for a twitter chat with EPA's water chief on tomorrow at 2pm EDT. Use #cleanwater to participate and submit questions.

Source: U.S. Environmental Protection Agency, [Twitter update], n.d., http://twitter.com/#!/EPAgov/status/71587196460736512.

Figure 9.5
A CDC_eHealth Tweet.

Source: Centers for Disease Control and Prevention, [Twitter update], n.d., http://twitter.com/#!/CDC_eHealth/status/71228762536161280.

Figure 9.6
A White House Tweet Including a #Follow Friday Example.

> **The White House**
> @whitehouse
> 🐦 Follow
>
> #followfriday Official info on H1N1:
> @CDCemergency @CDC_eHealth @whonews
> @BirdFluGov @dhsjournal @usedgov Thanks for
> the positive feedback!

Source: The White House, [Twitter update], n.d., http://twitter.com/#!/whitehouse/status/1674999496.

use the *list* feature to organize important Twitter accounts and quickly access only their updates in a targeted search. You can add account names to the list—even accounts you don't follow—and give the list a unique name. Note also that Twitter users can remove themselves from a list you have created. For example, the U.S. Environmental Protection Agency (EPA) is hosting more than twenty Twitter accounts in order to accommodate its diverse audiences (Figure 9.7).[5] Instead of following all twenty accounts, you could add them to a list and label the list, "All EPA Twitter accounts." In turn, you can follow other users' lists instead of following someone directly, and still get the updates that you deem relevant.

For many agencies, 140 characters (the maximum allowed in a tweet) are not enough to convey the message they want to send. Agencies have found creative ways to use tweets to point their followers to longer blog updates or to supply links to other media, such as press releases on the official government website or photo-sharing services, such as Flickr or yfrog. This practice has spurred the creation and use of *URL shorteners*, online services that reduce long URLs to very short links that can be inserted into a tweet. Popular services are for example TinyURL.com and Bit.ly. The official U.S. Government URL shortener service, Go.USA.gov, helps "government employees create short.gov URLs from official government domains, such as .gov, .mil, .si.edu, or .fed.us URLs."[6]

Twitter, like Facebook, has become a *social search engine*. People tend to pay attention to the updates within their own self-determined networks. To understand

Figure 9.7
The EPA Region 9 Twitter List.

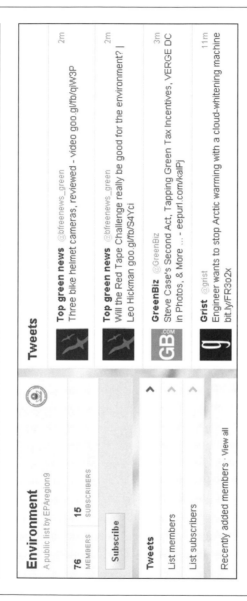

Source: U.S. Environmental Protection Agency, [Twitter update], n.d., http://twitter.com/#!/EPAregion9/environment.

what your constituencies or your audience members are talking about, you can use Twitter's powerful search mechanism: twitter.com/search. This search tool can be used to search in several different ways: for specific keywords or hashtags (using the # sign) and for people (in case you don't know their Twitter account name), organizations, or events. The search function gives you an easy way to "listen in" to ongoing conversations, which can help you monitor how your own organization or a hot topic of your agency is mentioned on Twitter. Even if you opt out of participating in social media services such as Twitter, that doesn't mean that your constituencies are not talking about you. The search tool will help you keep your finger on the conversational pulse, even if your agency chooses not to post content directly.

ADDITIONAL SUCCESSFUL PRACTICES

We strongly recommend that you *supply a disclaimer or a terms of service statement* on all official channels. For example, the White House Twitter account explicitly states that the messages may be archived, which means that they become part of the public record of the White House and should not be considered private messages. The statement says: "Official WH twitter account. Comments & messages received through official WH pages are subject to the PRA [Public Records Act] and may be archived. Learn more http://wh.gov/privacy [a link to the White House privacy page]." Many government agencies also use Twitter's "Bio" section to *identify who is tweeting*, thereby gaining additional information about that agency or individual.

Microblog Quick Start Guide

- Microblogs allow you to create brief text updates about your organization's news, events, and other public information. The brevity of microblogs creates challenges and opportunities that differentiate these services from full-scale blogs.

- Twitter is the best-known microblog service. It is used by governments to share news and information in an easily readable format.

- Many Twitter technologies and best practices have evolved to make Twitter an efficient tool for communication on both the agency and individual levels. (See the step-by-step guide earlier in this section for more detail.)

Wikis

Wikis are websites that can be easily modified by their users, without the use of technical skills or tools. Users can collaboratively create content, edit and change existing content, and discuss content with each other. *Wiki* is a Hawaiian word meaning "quick," and this name highlights the fact that wikis are easy and fast to edit.

Wikis are used to facilitate interaction and project collaboration. The most prominent wiki is Wikipedia, known as the world's online encyclopedia and founded in 2001 by Jimmy Wales to quickly create, edit, and change information on every term its contributors want to define. Authors can create a page on a specific topic and then publish a draft to the public, a draft that is open for edits and changes, and even deletion, by the whole world.

The original Wikipedia page is structured through *hyperlinks* that connect keywords used in one article to definitions provided in other articles. Definitions and other content are not supposed to be replicated in an article if they exist elsewhere in Wikipedia. Instead, authors are expected to provide links to the original pages.

The on-screen editor makes editing simple and easy (Figure 10.1). The formatting possibilities are reduced to a minimum of functions, and pages are not intended to be flashy or nicely decorated, with the result that the content of the page is the focus of authors and readers. Every registered user can edit content with a simple mouse click.

Disputes between authors can be discussed and tracked using the *discussion page*. It is wise for a new author or any editor to explain why he or she made changes and to provide an original source to support the changes and defend them against other authors, particularly on high-profile articles that are constantly monitored by authors who feel a sense of pride or ownership in

Figure 10.1
Edit Mode in Wikipedia.

Editing Social media

 You are not currently logged in. If you save any edits, your IP address will be recorded publicly in this page's edit history. If you create an account, you can conceal your IP address and be provided with many other benefits. Messages sent to your IP can be viewed on your talk page.

Please do not save test edits. If you want to experiment, please use the sandbox. If you need any help getting started with editing, see the New contributors' help page.

B *I* ▶ Advanced ▶ Special characters ▶ Help ▶ Cite

```
((Copy edit|date=July 2011))
[[File:Social Web Share Buttons.png|thumb|right|Examples of the share buttons common to many
social web pages]]
'''Social media''' includes web-based and mobile technologies used to turn [[communication]] into
interactive dialogue. Andreas Kaplan and Michael Haenlein define social media as "a group of
Internet-based applications that build on the ideological and technological foundations of [[Web
2.0]], and that allow the creation and exchange of [[user-generated content]]."<ref>((Cite journal
| doi = 10.1016/j.bushor.2009.09.003
| issn = 0007-6813
| volume = 53
| year = 2010
| issue = 1
| pages = 59-68
```

Source: Wikipedia, "Editing Social Media," n.d., http://en.wikipedia.org/w/index.php?title=Social_media&action=edit.

the content. In cases where multiple authors can't agree on changes made by another author, the article can automatically be reverted to the previous version. Content that is considered *off-topic* can be easily excluded from an article. The authors can also suggest that content needs to be reviewed by administrators, merged with other existing articles, or moved onto its own article page if it is of significant stand-alone value.

The original Wikipedia idea was to give editorial rights to every single person in the world, making Wikipedia a "democratic" content production site. Over time the community has evolved into a hierarchical editorial system, with several levels of access. In addition an informal culture has evolved in which some users perceive themselves as "article owners," reacting immediately to even the smallest changes random Internet surfers are making to their articles and correcting mistakes within minutes.

It became clear over time that the fear of vandalism—based on Wikipedia's open community structure and editorial system—was unsubstantiated. Although so-called Internet trolls who might try to vandalize an article always exist, the community is self-policing and very quick in responding to errors or reverting an article to its previously agreed-upon status. Overall, a few authors contribute a high number of articles, and the majority of the authors make only incremental changes.

A 2005 study published in *Nature* showed that Wikipedia comes close to the *Encyclopaedia Britannica* in terms of the accuracy of its science entries. Their error rates are comparable; however, the mistake elimination process shows a remarkable difference between the online and printed encyclopedias. Until the 2012 decision to stop producing a print edition of the *Encyclopaedia Britannica*, the printed version had been updated and reprinted about every four years, whereas Wikipedia authors are able to detect errors within four minutes on average and thus eliminate errors almost immediately.[1]

Wikipedia is built on wiki software called MediaWiki. Recently a host of other free wiki applications have emerged, such as PBworks, Socialtext, Wikia, Wetpaint, and Wikispaces. All of these freely available tools are similarly easy to navigate and to maintain. Each can be used as an open wiki or a closed system with restricted user access. Some wiki software applications offer an instant messaging service among the authors, blogging features, and other extensions supporting the collaborative process.[2]

USING WIKIS IN THE PUBLIC SECTOR

Wikis can be used as open information creation environments, such as Wikipedia, in which everyone can freely create collaborative content. Or they can be dedicated to a specific purpose, in which case authorship rights might be limited to specific authorized users. Some users might have a wiki for personal note-taking purposes; others might integrate a wiki into a corporate intranet as a full-fledged knowledge management system.

Yet another approach is to use a wiki to collect user-generated information. For example, WikiCrimes mashes content obtained from police logs with citizen input and geographical maps and displays numbers of crimes in specific regions (Figure 10.2).

Solutions such as WikiCrimes are based on the OpenStreetMap wiki that gathers and maps free geographical data, such as street locations, collected via a collaborative effort. OpenStreetMap was used for applications developed in the aftermath of the 2010 earthquake in Haiti to show relocated hospitals and emergency response locations.

Wikis are highly interactive tools. They allow single authorship, joint authorship, bidirectional exchanges, and interactivity in the production of content. In the current open government environment, they can be used as externally facing tools for sharing content with stakeholders in an effort to increase the transparency of processes, decision making, and information sharing. In addition, wikis allow citizens to interact with the content or to contribute their own content and discuss the current content and thus they are a way to increase participation in the public sector. Lastly, they can be used to support intra-, inter-, and extraorganizational collaboration and coordination of projects.

GETTING STARTED: WHEN, WHERE, AND WHY TO USE WIKIS

From our research we have identified three information-sharing situations in which wikis are typically used in the public sector: (a) within organizations, (b) across organizational units, and (c) with the public.

Information Sharing Within Organizations

Some wikis are used purely for internal knowledge creation and sharing purposes. Outsiders do not have access, and the wikis are used as parallel structures to existing information-sharing applications.

Figure 10.2
WikiCrimes: Mapping Crimes Collaboratively.

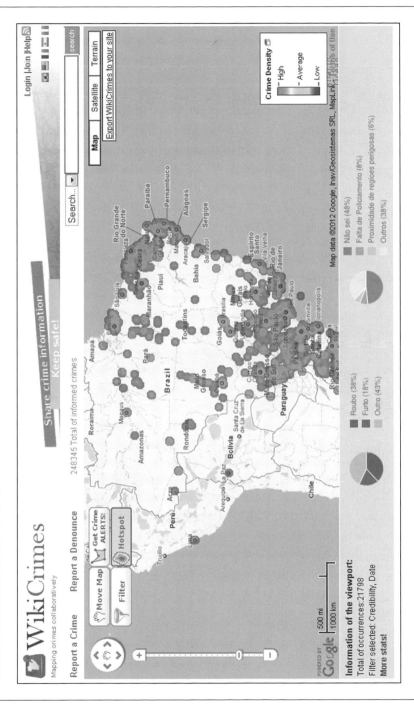

Source: WikiCrimes, [Crimes mapped for Brazil], 2011, http://wikicrimes.org. Used with the permission of WikiCrimes.

One public sector example made it to the front page of the *New York Times* a few years ago. In the process of rewriting its counterinsurgency manual, the U.S. Army used a wiki application to gather collaborative input from the authorized personnel involved in the revision effort.[3] With the assistance of this social media technology, the Army reached deep into its own organization to encourage participation and to accelerate the creation and sharing of knowledge.

One remarkable solution that is publicly accessible is the CrisisCommons wiki (Figure 10.3)—a collaborative management and teamwork wiki—and also see the description of the U.S. Army's Tactics, Techniques, and Procedures (TTP) wiki.[4]

Information Sharing Across Organizational Units

Some public sector wikis are set up to establish a shared collaboration and information-sharing environment for a number of agencies whose intranets are not connected.

As part of its Open Government Initiative, for example, the White House used a wiki it called ExpertNet, supported by Wikispaces, to collect ideas and opinions from the public about any topic the Office of Science and Technology Policy was then currently working on[5] (Figure 10.4).

Another example is GCPedia, the Government of Canada internal wiki that is used by government employees across all units of the Canadian government (Figure 10.5).

Information Sharing and Collaboration with Citizens

Government organizations can set up wikis to involve citizens in idea generation and policy definition processes. For example, a project of the City of San Jose, California, used Wikiplanning™ as part of the city's online solution to the problem of improving civic engagement in urban planning initiatives. The project team describes the Wikiplanning project as a *virtual charrette* for city planning (Figure 10.6).[6] The wiki was designed with the goal of incorporating the values of the community into decisions about major changes in the city's architecture and ensuring that the city was reflecting the values of the community in the plan that was developed. In general the wiki approach allowed the city to reach out to different neighborhood groups, businesses, and other stakeholders and to ask people to post information in the form of photographs or comments on a message board. Citizens were then allowed to ask and answer questions. The initial

Figure 10.3
The CrisisCommons Wiki for Organizing Disaster Relief.

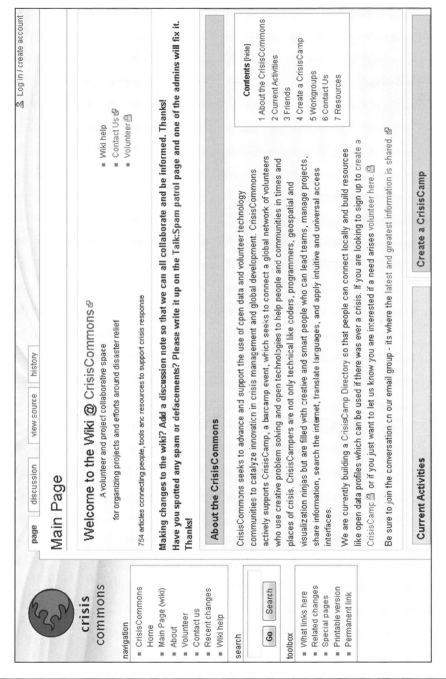

Source: CrisisCommons, "Main Page." n.d., http://wiki.crisiscommons.org/wiki/Main_Page. Used with the permission of CrisisCommons.

Figure 10.4
The White House Used the ExpertNet Wiki.

CIO.GOV

About | What We're Working On | News | Resources | CIO Council

INNOVATIONS

ExpertNet: The Federal Government Wants Your Answers

+ SHARE

Tags: ExpertNet, government wiki, collaboration platform, policymaking, citizen engagement, social media, crowdsourcing, transparency, citizen collaborators, best practices, White House Open Government Initiative, General Services Administration, GSA, Office of Management and Budget, OMB, Aneesh Chopra, Shelley Metzenbaum.

Comment Period Extended to January 23, 2011

How do you craft public policy questions that get genuinely useful responses from citizens? What's the best way to reach members of the public with the greatest expertise on a given topic? These are just some of the questions that the Government is seeking to answer as it develops ExpertNet (working title), a public-facing wiki platform.

ExpertNet is a collaborative effort between the White House Open Government

We are eager to hear about specific examples of tools that will achieve [the] goals outlined here" –

Search CIO.gov

Q Search CIO.Gov   GO ›

Related Blog Posts

Tuesday, March 6, 2012
Now Live: The Updated IT Dashboard
Steven VanRoekel, Federal CIO (from whitehouse.gov)

The Administration first launched the IT Dashboard back in 2009 as part of our effort to create a more transparent and open government. To…More ›

Friday, December 9, 2011
DOT: Leading the IPv6 Initiative
Nitin Pradhan, CIO, DOT (cio.gov)

The global Internet transition from IPv4 to IPv6 picked up significant momentum late last year with the OMB IPv6 Mandate (released in Septem…More ›

Source: The White House, "Background Information" [for ExpertNet], n.d., http://expertnet.wikispaces.com.

Figure 10.5
An Introductory Page on GCPedia.

Source: WordPress, 2010, http://spaghettitesting.files.wordpress.com/2010/04/gcpedia_main_e_2010-04-28.png.

submission process was open for a limited time, and citizens were invited to comment in a second phase on a selection of the submissions and to help with formulating the final policy documents.

Another great example is the U.S. General Services Administration's BetterBuy project, launched by Mary Davie. This is a pilot wiki project to allow vendors and government employees to collect information about upcoming acquisitions before the official requests for proposal are published, with the goal of improving process effectiveness and efficiency (Figure 10.7).

Figure 10.6
Wikiplanning™.

Source: Wikiplanning™, [Wikiplanning welcome page], n.d., http://www.wikiplanning.org. Used with the permission of Wikiplanning.

Figure 10.7
The GSA's BetterBuy Wiki Project.

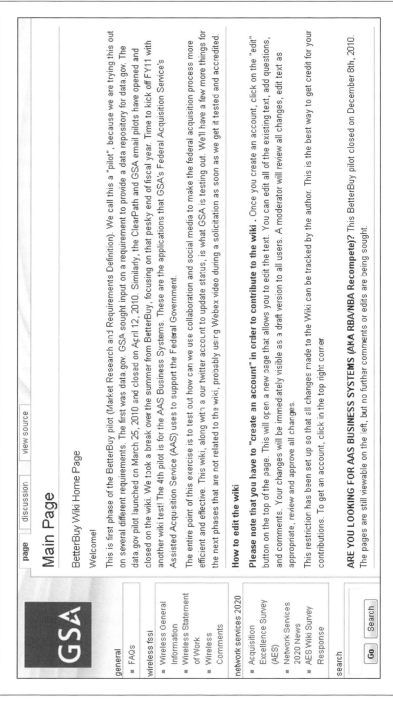

GSA

| page | discussion | view source |

Main Page

BetterBuy Wiki Home Page

Welcome!

This is first phase of the BetterBuy pilot (Market Research and Requirements Definition). We call this a "pilot", because we are trying this out on several different requirements. The first was data.gov. GSA sought input on a requirement to provide a data repository for data.gov. The data.gov pilot launched on March 25, 2010 and closed on April 12, 2010. Similarly, the ClearPath and GSA email pilots have opened and closed on the wiki. We took a break over the summer from BetterBuy, focusing on that pesky end of fiscal year. Time to kick off FY11 with another wiki test! The 4th pilot is for the AAS Business Systems. These are the applications that GSA's Federal Acquisition Service's Assisted Acquisition Service (AAS) uses to support the Federal Government.

The entire point of this exercise is to test out how can we use collaboration and social media to make the federal acquisition process more efficient and effective. This wiki, along with a our twitter account to update status, is what GSA is testing out. We'll have a few more things for the next phases that are not related to the wiki, probably using Webex video during a solicitation as soon as we get it tested and accredited.

How to edit the wiki

Please note that you have to "create an account" in order to contribute to the wiki. Once you create an account, click on the "edit" button on the top of the page. This will open a new page that allows you to edit the text. You can edit all of the existing text, add questions, and comments. Your changes will be immediately visible as a draft version to all users. A moderator will review all changes, edit text as appropriate, review and approve all changes.

This restriction has been set up so that all changes made to the Wiki can be tracked by the author. This is the best way to get credit for your contributions. To get an account, click in the top right corner

ARE YOU LOOKING FOR AAS BUSINESS SYSTEMS (AKA RBA/NBA Recompete)? This BetterBuy pilot closed on December 8th, 2010. The pages are still viewable on the left, but no further comments or edits are being sought.

general
- FAQs

wireless fssi
- Wireless General Information
- Wireless Statement of Work
- Wireless Comments

network services 2020
- Acquisition Excellence Survey (AES)
- Network Services 2020 News
- AES Wiki Survey Response

search

[ ] [Go] [Search]

Source: U. S. General Services Administration, "BetterBuy Wiki Home Page," 2010, https://betterbuy.fas.gsa.gov/index.php/Main_Page.

Wiki Quick Start Guide

We suggest a step-by-step process when you start using wikis in the public sector.

- Start with a small wiki centered on a small, internal project. Get your hands dirty, and experiment with the collaborative writing experience. See how it evolves, and experiment with the process.

- When you've gained a reasonable comfort level with the tools, open up this wiki to your whole department or to a peer agency or another government organization before going directly to the public with the tool set. Using this methodical process will help you achieve in-house buy-in and create the cultural change needed for a new tool set and approach to collaboration and communication to be used effectively.

- Once you have done this, you can begin to experiment with public access to your wiki. San Jose's thoughtful approach to deploying a planning wiki may be a productive model to consider.

Choosing the Tool That's Right for You

So how will you know which tool set is right for you? There are literally hundreds of social media applications available today, and no doubt there will be a hundred more in the years to come. Because of the rapid rise and malleable nature of many of these tools, we are not able to capture them all in the confines of this book. But the tools we have discussed here will certainly give you a taste of the most recognizable social media technologies used in government today.

If you've got a new idea, chances are someone, somewhere, has already done what you want to do—there is no need to reinvent the wheel. Research and refine existing tools until you find out exactly what works for you! Build on the ideas and processes that others have found to be successful. Start your social media adventures with small, controlled experiments. Mix and match the tools to the purpose and audience you have in mind.

You can also make your social media presence more engaging and useful by using other applications to enhance your content. Consider adding a photo stream to your blog posts. Attract new followers by providing your blog postings in an audio file via podcasts. Reference digitized documents and other web resources to increase the reach of your wiki. Create links to relevant video content on YouTube from your microblogging or social network service account to draw a larger audience. If a picture is worth a thousand words, think how valuable a full video could be! There are also time-saving tools (for example, HootSuite or TweetDeck) that will help you manage multiple services by coordinating content to and from a single interface, and there are services (for example, RSS feeds) that enable you to automate the process of sharing content across multiple platforms. Once you are accustomed to the tool set that meets your needs, you can explore these add-ons to *increase* the communication impact of your social media tools and *decrease* their care and feeding requirements.

MATCHING TOOLS TO NEEDS MATRIX

Table 11.1 is a weighted matrix displaying the potential value of the major types of social media tools in relation to the most common general service needs of a government organization (with ✓ representing a relatively low value and ✓✓✓ a relatively high value).

In Section Seventeen we will take a look at some of the social tools, such as innovation platforms and virtual worlds, that are also gaining ground as resources for government organizations.

ADDITIONAL RESOURCES

For assistance with selecting your tool set, we also recommend reviewing the HowTo .gov website (Figure 11.1), hosted by the U.S. General Services Administration and managed by GSA's Office of Citizen Services and Innovative Technologies and the Federal Web Managers Council. HowTo.gov provides guidance on selecting the right social media application for your needs. Click on "Social Media" to select the type of social media application you would like to use. You will be directed to a web page for each social media tool; for example, if you want to use a blog, you'll be directed to www.howto.gov/social-media/blogs. On that blog page, you will find a way to check whether you need a blog and information about how to develop a strategic plan, how to determine the resources you need to maintain the blog, how to chose the right blog tool, how to train your employees, how to develop metrics to measure your success, and how to set up use policies.

Another valuable resource to review is the Government & Social Media Wiki. It functions as a central hub for information and practical examples on how government organizations can use social media applications (Figure 11.2).

The case example that closes this section illustrates how the Boynton Beach, Florida, Police Department uses several social media tools to help it achieve its mission and involve local citizens in public safety.

Table 11.1
Matching Social Media Tools to Common Government Needs.

	SOCIAL NETWORKING PLATFORMS (FOR EXAMPLE, FACEBOOK)	BLOGS (FOR EXAMPLE, WORDPRESS)	MICROBLOGS (FOR EXAMPLE, TWITTER)	WIKIS (FOR EXAMPLE, MEDIAWIKI)
Public information (announcements)	✓✓✓	✓✓✓	✓✓✓	✓
Public education	✓✓	✓✓	✓✓	✓✓✓
Surveys and public input requests	✓✓✓	✓✓	✓✓	✓✓✓
Event planning and management	✓✓✓	✓✓✓	✓	✓✓✓
Emergency preparedness	✓	✓✓✓	✓✓	✓✓✓
Resource and volunteer coordination	✓✓	✓✓	✓✓	✓✓
Emergency response	✓✓✓	✓	✓✓✓	✓✓
Peer networking	✓✓✓			✓✓✓
Employee and volunteer recruiting	✓✓✓	✓✓	✓✓✓	✓✓✓
Advertising, marketing, and tourism	✓✓✓	✓✓		✓✓✓
Economic development		✓✓✓		✓✓✓
Project management		✓✓✓		✓✓✓
Hazard and traffic advisories	✓✓	✓✓	✓✓✓	
Complaint and problem reporting	✓✓✓	✓	✓✓	

Figure 11.1
HowTo.gov.

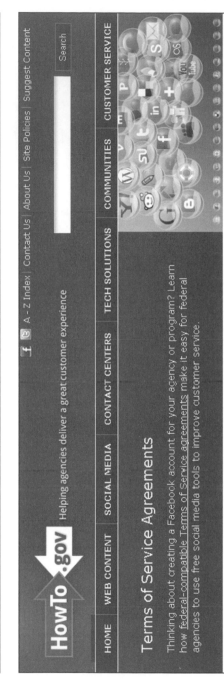

HowTo .gov Helping agencies deliver a great customer experience

HOME | WEB CONTENT | SOCIAL MEDIA | CONTACT CENTERS | TECH SOLUTIONS | COMMUNITIES | CUSTOMER SERVICE

A - Z Index | Contact Us | About Us | Site Policies | Suggest Content

Search

Terms of Service Agreements

Thinking about creating a Facebook account for your agency or program? Learn how federal-compatible Terms of Service agreements make it easy for federal agencies to use free social media tools to improve customer service.

Web Content

Federal web requirements, content management, usability, analytics, accessibility, web writing, search...

Social Media

Terms of Service agreements, new media, video, social networks, blogs, challenges & contests...

UPCOMING EVENTS

Apr 11–12	Writing for the Web Workshop
Mar 20	Usability Testing and Debriefing Best Practices
Mar 21	First Fridays Product Testing
May 16–17	2012 Government Web and New Media Conference

More Training »

WHAT'S NEW

Source: HowTo.gov, [Web page], n.d., http://www.howto.gov.

Figure 11.2

The Government & Social Media Wiki.

Main Page

Welcome to the Government & Social Media Wiki

Hi, my name is Josh Shpayher ⊡ and this is my website which aims to help Congress, elected officials and their staffs from the Hill and around the country and the world, the media, and the public at large track who in government uses which forms of Social Media. Keep checking back as I will be constantly adding new offices of federal, state and local government, campaigns, and government agencies.

The Government and Social Media blog can be found at blog.govsm.com ⊡ Check there for regular page announcements as well as other government and social media news and info. Don't forget to sign up for the RSS ⊡ feed.

Please follow me on 🅣 @govsm ⊡, 🖰, 🇫, or 🅻 use the discussion pages, and come back often!

Contents [hide]

1 Announcements
2 Getting Started
   2.1 Federal Government
   2.2 State and Local Government
   2.3 Other Pages
3 New Pages
4 Coming Soon
5 Feedback
6 What They're Saying
7 Congress Twitter Feed

Announcements

- My interview about the Whipcast app with Jared Rizzi on *The Morning Briefing*, Sirius/XM's POTUS channel on November 21st.

- Video of my speech from the iima4gov conference in Sacramento: http://iima4gov.org/conference-video ⊡

Source: Government & Social Media Wiki, 'Welcome page], n.d., http://govsm.com.

Stephanie H. Slater

Public Information Officer

Boynton Beach (FL) Police Department

BOYNTON BEACH, FL—Five years ago, Boynton Beach Police Chief Matt Immler created a community policing initiative focused on identifying and addressing criminal elements plaguing neighborhoods in the city.

Part of his initiative was tackling the public's perception, due to a myriad of issues including lack of effective communication, that the police department was not doing enough to keep its community safe.

Here is how a small law enforcement agency on the southeast coast of Florida used Social Media to transform its reputation and regain the community's support.

The Boynton Beach Police Department (BBPD) is located in Palm Beach County, about 15 miles south of West Palm Beach. The BBPD, which employs 164 sworn officers and about 55 civilians, serves a population of approximately 75,000 residents.

We were the first law enforcement agency in the state to use Social Media to inform, educate and engage the community. We began using YouTube in September 2007, followed by MySpace and then Facebook in April 2008. We joined the Twitterverse in September 2009.

When we began using Social Media, it was around the time that the journalism industry was starting to cut its staff significantly and transition into a 24-hour news cycle. No longer were they breaking news in the print edition every morning. It was happening as the news happened, in real time and online.

It was becoming [increasingly] difficult to get media coverage of "the little things" that were important to the department and neighborhood groups or local businesses but not the story of the day for TV or worthy of taking up inches in the newspaper.

The BBPD then decided to use Social Media to become its own news outlet, essentially allowing us to tell the public anything and everything we wanted them to know, and ensuring that they got the message we intended for them to receive. Posting original press releases and videos of press conferences in their entirety on Facebook and YouTube also allowed us to hold the media accountable for their reporting.

For most people, their interaction with police is usually not under the best of circumstances. It's often when they have been victimized or they find themselves on the other side of the law. Social Media allows law enforcement to show people another side of the badge. But if your agency is going to start a relationship with the community online, you must be prepared to work at it. You need to consistently interact with them. That means posting items on Facebook or Tweeting on a daily basis.

The BBPD is constantly updating Social Media with press releases, photographs of suspects who need to be identified, upcoming events or programs such as the Citizens Police Academy, congratulatory items such as agency promotions or Officer of the Month awards and videos of press conferences. Sometimes we even pat ourselves on the backs by posting videos or links to positive news coverage.

A key component is talking to the community online. We solicit information about criminal activity plaguing their neighborhoods, and we routinely respond to the questions and comments they post on our page or tweet to us. In the coming months, we'll be expanding our online efforts through live web chats with our police chief via Facebook, Twitter and Ustream.

Law enforcement agencies should also be using Social Media as a resource in criminal investigations, for conducting background checks on potential employees and studying crime trends.

Recently, we posted surveillance photos on Facebook of a woman using someone else's credit card to buy thousands of dollars in merchandise from a local retailer. Several days later, the woman contacted police and admitted to committing the crime. A friend told her she was wanted by police after seeing her photo on BBPD's Facebook.

There are now 2,265 people who like us on Facebook and 2,906 who follow us on Twitter. Our YouTube videos have been viewed more than 2 million times. We've also found that most people looking for information about the BBPD go to Facebook before they go to our website, www.bbpd .org. We believe this to be the case now for most law enforcement agencies.

We turned to social media to humanize our police officers and open the doors of the department to its residents to let them see, hear and be a part of everything we do on a daily basis.

Judging by the kudos posted on our Facebook wall and the #FF (Follow Fridays) on Twitter, we're confident in our partnership with a community that knows we're doing everything we can to keep them safe.

Thank-you messages like this one have become commonplace on BBPD's Facebook. The officers appreciate knowing that their efforts are making a difference.

Source: Used with the permission of Boynton Beach Police Department, Boynton Beach, Florida.

An example of content on the BBPD's Facebook page:

The Live Web Chat with Chief Immler via Facebook, Twitter and
Ustream is an example of our latest online initiative:

Cross-promotion with COPS. The TV show is riding with our officers
this season.

Source: Used with the permission of Boynton Beach Police Department, Boynton Beach, Florida.

Engagement is a critical component to our Facebook use. We try to address every comment or question posted on our wall:

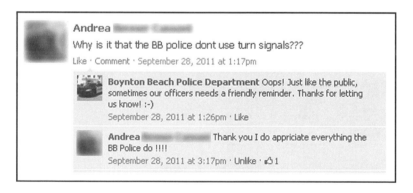

Source: Used with the permission of Boynton Beach Police Department, Boynton Beach, Florida.

PART THREE

Policy and Implementation

Social Media: Federal Agencies Need Policies and Procedures for Managing and Protecting Information They Access and Disseminate

—Title of a GAO report[1]

In this section of our field guide we focus on the actual implementation tasks. We will guide you step-by-step through the process of getting your social media presence up to speed. We will first highlight the main elements of a social media strategy and policy document and offer best practices examples from government organizations on the federal, state, and local levels. After that we'll show how you and your agency can get started and set up social media procedures and processes that have proven successful in other agencies.

Social Media Strategy

In this section we will focus on the strategies to consider as you move forward. It is crucial to note that the following components are typically not developed one after another but in an overlapping fashion. You will likely have to consider some aspects simultaneously in order to meet the specific and current needs of your organization and the focus of your social media efforts.

In the midst of the current explosion of social media use among government agencies, previous guidelines and technology standards do not apply. Rules and norms will not have a chance to truly coalesce until the evolution of technologies and platforms and the ways in which these can be used become somewhat less fluid. Some agencies have therefore put an initial hold on using social media in order to wait for new guidance. Others, however, have dived in headfirst and created use or business cases in a relative policy vacuum. Many of these agencies have come up with written strategy or policy documents that can be characterized as *rolling documents*—as soon as there are changes in the platforms (which happens often) or there are unintended consequences in the form of changed user behavior, these agencies update their policy documents to reflect their current social media use. An incident involving a U.S. congressman in 2011 produced a prominent example of policy change resulting from unintended consequences. As a result of Representative Anthony Wiener's inappropriate distribution of pictures on Twitter, members of Congress changed their guidelines on the use of Twitter.[1]

As the use of social media in government increases, the need for rules, regulations, and standardization at both the federal and agency levels has increased as well. Agencies are now documenting their need for agency-specific rules for their day-to-day management of their diverse social media accounts in documents that they refer to as social media handbooks, social media strategy, policy for the use of social media, or linking strategy. All of these documents have one goal in common: to help guide the behavior of those employees responsible for populating social media accounts. But they also often extend beyond the official use of social media to include awareness-building components that address the responsible and professional use of social media by all public sector employees. We'll talk more about the personal use of social media by employees in Section Fifteen. Regardless of what it is called, your social media strategy should focus on the big picture of social media within your organization. What does your agency expect to get out of social media use? How will you integrate this use into the overall strategy of the organization?

We suggest that you will answer these questions most successfully if you first identify your organization's mission and understand who its audiences are and how these audiences are currently interacting on social media channels. With these insights to guide your decision making, you can draft your social media strategy to include the most appropriate and necessary tools, day-to-day practices, and standards and rules.

FOCUSING ON MISSION SUPPORT

All communication and social media tasks should be well aligned with your government organization's mission. The mission states the motivation or general objective of your government organization. Most agencies can align all tasks, activities, and outputs within the framework of their overall mission. Some agencies post their mission statements prominently on the front page of their web presence. Take for example the mission statement of the U.S. Environmental Protection Agency (EPA). It is highlighted on the right-hand side of the agency's front page: "EPA's mission is to protect human health and the environment" (Figure 12.1). Elsewhere on its website, the agency describes the actions it takes to accomplish its mission and what is involved in those actions. The basic activities are to[2]

- Develop and enforce regulations
- Give grants
- Study environmental issues
- Sponsor partnerships

Figure 12.1
The EPA's Mission Statement.

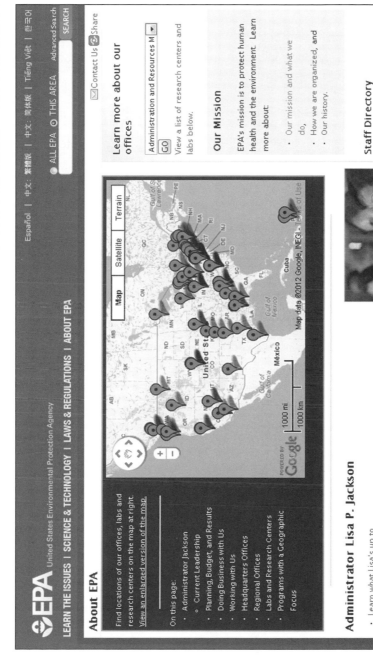

Source: U.S. Environmental Protection Agency, "Our Mission and What We Do," n.d., http://www.epa.gov/aboutepa/whatwedo.html.

- Teach people about the environment
- Publish information

Using the boundaries outlined by this mission statement, it is easy to draw parallels and identify the ways in which social media outreach and connectivity could further the stated agency mission.

IDENTIFYING YOUR ORGANIZATION'S AUDIENCES

The fundamental value for government agencies of using social media is the ability they gain to generate and maintain a civil online discourse. Crowdsourcing cannot occur where no one gathers, where there are no friends, followers, or fans. Diversity of opinion and frequent feedback are positive signs when an agency is seeking feedback and ideas for development. Building an audience, increasing followers and *likes*, enables your agency to continue to broadcast its message to a widening circle of interested constituencies. Frequent, relevant interaction, coupled with an ever-increasing ring of participants, creates a communication snowball effect that leads to ever greater participation as content is recycled, repurposed, and regenerated in an ongoing cycle. Simply put, the more you message and the more people you message with, the further the message goes and the more valuable and relevant the output becomes.

Social media strategy is based on the mission statement. It is necessary to understand how the use of social media can advance your agency's activities. A first step is to identify the strategic communication and interaction objectives. For example, consider again the activities the EPA carries out to accomplish its mission. Several of these activities are described as having specific communication needs, as shown in Table 12.1.

As the communication and interaction objectives reveal, the EPA has a diverse set of audiences. Policymakers; state, local, and tribal government representatives; nonprofits; educational institutions; state laboratories; program partners; and the general public participate in the information-sharing and collaborative opportunities. Although the EPA certainly has a unique mission and provides specific scientific information, it is very similar to other government organizations when it comes to audiences. No government organization has just one specific audience—some might not have a broad audience, such as the general public, but most government organizations interact with many

Table 12.1
The EPA's Strategic Communication and Interaction Objectives.

TASKS AND ACTIVITIES	OBJECTIVES
Develop and enforce regulations	Interact with and inform *policymakers*, *state representatives*, and *tribal governments*, as well as *companies* that have to adhere to new regulations.
Give grants	Communicate the availability of grants to *state environmental programs*, *nonprofit organizations*, *educational institutions*, and so forth.
Study environmental issues	Collaborate with *laboratories*, share information with *other countries*, *private sector organizations*, *academic institutions*, and *other agencies*.
Sponsor partnerships	Support partnerships with *businesses*, *nonprofit organizations*, and *state and local governments*. In return, the EPA shares information and publicly recognizes the partners.
Teach people about the environment	Teach *everyone* about responsible use of the environment.

Source: Table adapted from the EPA's mission statement, http://www.epa.gov/aboutepa/whatwedo.html.

different types of constituencies and provide access and information to many different recipients.

The city of Hampton, Virginia, outlines its diverse audiences in the purpose portion of its social media policy: "City of Hampton departments may utilize social media and social network sites to *further enhance communications with various stakeholder organizations in support of City goals and objectives.* City officials and City organizations have the ability to publish articles, facilitate discussions and communicate information through various media related to conducting City business. *Social media facilitates further discussion of City issues, operations and services by providing members of the public the opportunity to participate in many ways* using the Internet [emphasis added]."[3]

Many agencies have reported that they developed a social media audience by reviewing the most popular social networking services and deciding to set up accounts based simply on the number of users already enrolled in Facebook, Twitter, YouTube, and so on. Once an organization establishes a social media presence on a particular platform, it can begin to measure how effective the tool is in helping it to achieve its stated mission and reach its defined audiences. We have observed two distinct approaches to identifying the right social media tools:

1. *The shotgun approach.* Organizations using the shotgun approach try to do everything. They are populating all available social media channels but doing little to inquire about and focus efforts on audience members' needs and preferred ways of interacting with government.

2. *The less is more approach.* Organizations using this approach do not let themselves get overwhelmed by the sheer number of social media tools and the pressure to populate all of them at once. Instead, they settle down and look specifically at where their audiences are.

We believe that the less is more approach will prove to be a more effective use of your agency's time and resources. We'll talk more in Section Sixteen about conducting your own controlled experiments to learn what you need and what works.

BUILDING YOUR ORGANIZATION'S AUDIENCES

There are several common methods governments use to develop social media audiences:

1. *Establish a useful presence.* The first step is to implement your chosen social media tools in the areas where your constituents already live. Create a social networking account. Begin filling it with information valued by your desired audience. If you want to attract constituents of your agency, begin publishing content that they will find useful (events, news updates, policy changes).

2. *Provide opportunities for input.* Pose questions, encourage suggestions, and solicit feedback. This can be direct. For example, you might send a tweet: "It's time to repaint the downtown lampposts. Let us know what color you prefer—or complete our online survey: [*survey hyperlink here*]." Or it

can be indirect. For example, you might use Facebook to invite users to an event: "Join us this Thursday at 5:30 PM at the Central Library to voice your opinion on the location for the new branch library."

3. *Be responsive.* When soliciting input, be sure to reply to all responses in a timely and helpful manner. Even if you don't consider the responses ideal, take all responses seriously and react accordingly. This demonstrates (in a visible forum) your organization's recognition and acceptance of the ongoing dialogue as a valuable tool.

4. *Encourage content sharing.* Ask your agency's followers to help you get the message out, particularly for important or timely information. Encourage them to share your information with their own circle of contacts.

5. *Incorporate social media outlets into your traditional outlets.* Once you have established solid roots in one or more social media platforms, reminding people about them through the agency's traditional communication channels should become common practice. They should be prominent on your organization's website and letterhead. Advertise them on your marquees and television stations and programs. Hang posters in heavily trafficked areas of counter service. Stock up on inexpensive giveaways for community events (pencils, magnets, and the like) that advertise your social media services. However your organization solicits feedback, incorporate your social media channels into that as well: "For more information, call us, visit our website, or follow us on Twitter."

Social Media Strategy Summary Review

Here are our recommendations on how to get started:

- Identify the need and weigh that need against the potential values and methods available within the tool sets described in Section Eleven.

- Define your goals, your success criteria, and the audience you need to reach.

- Balance the potential risks and rewards. Popular ideas and hot topics can quickly take on a viral life of their own when you get them online.

- Reevaluate the process from time to time to be sure the focus is still on target. If a strategy doesn't work, toss it out and try something new!

Social Media Tactics

Your social media tactics will help to guide your agency's activities and tasks. We suggest looking into the following four tactics to determine which ones might be most helpful in supporting your agency's mission.

INFORMATION AND EDUCATION TACTIC

In the previous section we presented the U.S. Environmental Agency's mission statement and supporting activities. It is clear from the EPA's discussion of its mission that large parts of putting it into action are focused on pushing information out to different audiences to inform and educate them (Figure 13.1). This includes publishing information about upcoming grant proposals, disseminating results of the newest research, and advertising and highlighting the work of partner organizations. This tactic purely pushes information out through a variety of channels, including social media channels. Similarly much of the information published on your organization's website can be recycled and channeled to your Facebook and Twitter followers. This tactic has the advantage of potentially reaching those members of your audience who don't have a daily incentive to visit your website and who prefer to receive your updates in their Facebook newsfeed or Twitter stream.

CITIZEN PARTICIPATION AND ENGAGEMENT THROUGH COMMUNITY BUILDING TACTIC

A more sophisticated social media tactic is the *pull tactic*, designed to pull audience members into your agency's communication process and engage them with your content.[1] The underlying logic here is that the crowd is more knowledgeable than a single government agency and might be able to help develop new

Figure 13.1
A Purely Informational EPA Twitter Update.

U.S. EPA @EPAgov   1h
#PoisonPrevent Tip: Poisonings are preventable! Read the label
before using pesticides & household products, 1.usa.gov/ygC9UF

Source: U.S. Environmental Protection Agency, [Twitter update], n.d., http://twitter.com/#!/EPAgov/status/97057825850793985.

ideas, share existing knowledge, or even provide its own crowdsourced content.[2] A prominent recent example involves the Facebook and Twitter town hall meetings run by President Obama in April and July 2011 (Figure 13.2). Both online town hall meetings included a phase during which members of the public submitted their questions for the president to answer. Using the Twitter hashtag **#askobama** and the Twitter site askobama.twitter.com, citizens submitted over 70,000 questions. The town hall meeting was broadcast live on YouTube and Facebook video, and the play-by-play status was live-tweeted on Twitter. Following the event the White House posted summaries, transcripts, and videos on its website (www.whitehouse.gov) for those who were not able to attend.

NETWORKING TACTIC

Building a network among your agency's audience members and simply listening in or helping to connect people to each other to discuss issues constitutes the most difficult social media tactic. The U.S. General Services Administration (GSA) used the informal social networking site GovLoop.com to create a social media discussion around the GSA's Acquisition 2.0 effort. These discussions, populated by a diverse audience of government employees, led to the creation of the BetterBuy wiki project (betterbuy.fas.gsa.gov), which transformed the GSA's multibillion-dollar acquisition process. Requests for proposals (RFPs) are now crowdsourced, meaning that vendors and agencies submit suggested revisions to an RFP before the agency officially releases it for solicitation. Mary Davie, assistant commissioner of the GSA Office of Integrated Technology Services, was able

Figure 13.2

Facebook and Twitter Town Hall Meeting.

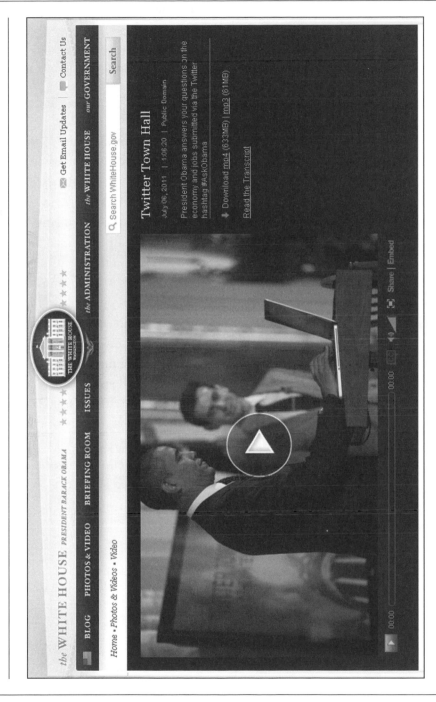

to form a tribe of government employees, journalists, students, and vendors who were knowledgeable about purchasing processes and willing to discuss the GSA's need, and they came up with an innovation that helps the agency to be more effective and efficient in its acquisition of goods and services (Figure 13.3).

TRANSACTIONAL SOCIAL MEDIA TACTIC

The newest tactic evolving today moves beyond networking into a transactional form of interaction, in which agencies use social media channels as a conduit that enables users to conduct routine business tasks: a user provides specific and explicit information with the expectation of a tangible result. This will be a new channel of service, in which agencies provide self-service mechanisms to constituents, allowing them to request services and information via social media channels. We liken this to the rise of *e-government* services in the early 2000s, services that are now ubiquitous. Governments opened access to common services via websites. They created an extensive online presence and put tools in the hands of consumers, via online transactional systems that enabled users to self-manage online payments, database queries, and service requests. Using *transactional social media* follows the same concept but moves the transactions into the social space—once again, following the crowds to be where the people are.

Agencies have recognized that constituents are now more mobile and more social, and they've found ways to capitalize on the new threads of communication offered via social media. In February of 2011, for example, the City of San Francisco launched an integrated service request system that allows citizens to report common problems, such as graffiti and damaged sidewalks, without ever leaving Facebook. Submitted complaints are routed to the city's 311 customer service center for resolution (Figure 13.4).

San Francisco Mayor Ed Lee recognized the value of the social media connection in a news release about the new service: "With nearly 260,000 fans of the City and County of San Francisco, it was necessary to create a better tool to enhance the public experience to connect with our City and report issues through our 311 system so we can take action," said Mayor Lee. "Social media like Facebook and Twitter have enhanced the public experience for our residents, connected communities, and transformed neighborhoods and businesses."[3]

Figure 13.3
GovLoop: The BetterBuy Project and Acquisition 2.0.

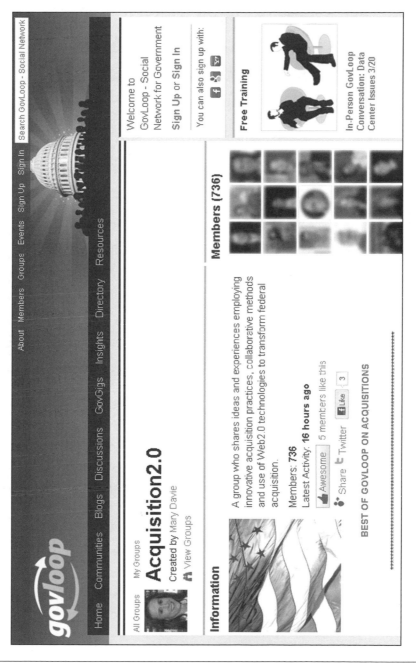

Source: GovLoop, Acquisition 2.0, n.d., http://www.govloop.com/group/acquisition20.

Figure 13.4
San Francisco's Service Request System on Facebook.

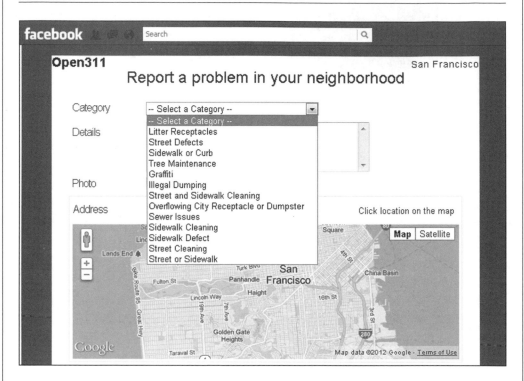

Source: The City and County of San Francisco, San Francisco 311 Customer Service Center, n.d., https://www
.facebook.com/SF311.

Key Elements of a Social Media Policy

Many government agencies have an established, social media *policy* document, created to guide the use of social media within the organization. Many of these documents acknowledge the fact that the document is a flexible, *rolling* guide, updated as necessary in order to maintain relevancy. Social media platform providers constantly innovate and change their platforms, and social media users often can manage the flow and use of platforms as they see fit. The wisdom and direction of crowds can greatly affect the evolution and use of the tools. This makes it imperative that social media policies be nimble enough to adhere to and take advantage of the newest developments and trends. This fluid situation can put a significant burden on your agency. Such policies demand constant care and feeding of your social media channels, and that will require you to stay up-to-date and look ahead at the ongoing changes that might affect your agency's use of a platform. In this section, we will walk you through the main topics typically covered in a social media policy document. (GovLoop maintains a self-updating list of social media policy and strategy documents for public access).[1]

The focus of most social media policies is to provide clear guidance on how to use social media applications as official communication mechanisms for public engagement. Some agencies clearly state the purpose and type of content that is acceptable for publishing via social media channels; others leave the purpose open and simply state that the tools are to be used responsibly and *for legitimate business purposes only*.[2] (In Section Fifteen, we'll cover the personal use of social media and the impacts of personal use in the workplace.) The degree of regulation and standard setting varies widely across government organizations. Some policies provide explicit guidance for day-to-day tasks. Other policies set only the initial framework or context in which departments and their agencies should use social media, as the example of the *Navy Command Social Media Handbook*, shown in Figure 14.1, illustrates.[3]

DEFINING ORGANIZATIONAL RESPONSIBILITY

We have observed that social media activities in government are emerging either as bottom-up initiatives spearheaded by individuals passionate about the potential the applications are providing or as a concerted effort of a specific department that is traditionally in charge of public engagement initiatives or technology in general. In Section Sixteen we will discuss the value and importance of establishing an initial social media workgroup that can use targeted, controlled experiments to demonstrate the value of social media. This group can be the spearhead of an organization-wide initiative, garnering interest in and support for the use of social media as a common practice. But the more social media use is evolving and taking shape in government organizations, the more important it becomes to allocate resources and define responsibilities to integrate the activities into the standard operating procedures as a formal and permanent strategy. Otherwise the initial activities may run out of steam— particularly if they are not recognized as an important resource for engagement and information dissemination and as tools to support the organization's mission.

Long-term responsibility for social media efforts in government is often assigned to an agency's technology department—already in charge of technology in government—or a public affairs or citizen communication unit. Assigning this initiative often depends on the focus of your social media strategy (see Section Twelve for the different pathways that are available) and the size and culture of your organization or your business units. Some agencies, particularly those that ventured into social media use early, have evolved their strategy and now make social media the responsibility of "everyone." A recent decision at the Department of Defense was to abandon the role of the social media director and instead transfer that position's responsibilities onto many shoulders in the organization.[4] It is very difficult for a single department or division to speak with the knowledge and authority of all the business units of an organization. "Official" responses often require time and research. They frequently result in formal

Figure 14.1
Sample Pages from the *Navy Command Social Media Handbook*.

Checklist for Establishing a Command Social Media Presence

CONSIDERATIONS FOR AN OFFICIAL COMMAND SOCIAL MEDIA PRESENCE

☐ **AUDIENCE**
· Identify who you are interested in communicating to and on what social media site(s) you can use to best reach them.

☐ **BRANDING**
· The name of your social media presence is critical; this is how people will find you. Follow the guidelines contained in the Social Media Snapshot on brand management to select the most appropriate name.

☐ **CONTENT**
· Think about the kind of content you intend to post and how frequently you intend to post – including responses to those expressing themselves on your site.

☐ **MANAGEMENT**
· Identify a team of people to manage the social media presence(s). Your trust in them and their good judgment are paramount.
· A diverse team managing the page will be more effective than a single person. A single manager is a single point of failure.

☐ **POLICY & TRAINING**
· Establish a policy to include business rules on how your team will manage the social media presence(s). Hold them to it.
· Train your personnel and their families on the safe and responsible use of social media and what they can expect from your social media presences.
· A good resource for policy and training can be found at www.slideshare.net/USNavySocialMedia

Navy Command Social Media Handbook - Fall 2010

10

REQUIREMENTS FOR AN OFFICIAL COMMAND SOCIAL MEDIA PRESENCE

☐ **COMMANDING OFFICER OR PUBLIC AFFAIRS OFFICER APPROVAL**
· Someone with release authority for the command must approve

☐ **THE POC MUST INCLUDE A VALID .MIL ADDRESS WHEN SUBMITTING**
· Only exception is if submission is from a command authorized to use .edu or .com

☐ **THE PRESENCE MUST HAVE A URL TO AN OFFICIAL DON WEBSITE**
· Your command's or in the absence of a command site www.navy.mil

☐ **THE PRESENCE MUST POST DISCLAIMER TEXT (REQUIRED)**
· The disclaimer identifies the page as an official DON social media presence and disclaims any endorsement
· An approved disclaimer is available at http://www.chinfo.navy.mil/socialmedia/user_agreement.doc

☐ **THE PRESENCE MUST HAVE A USER AGREEMENT (AS APPROPRIATE)**
· The user agreement establishes what is acceptable criteria for posts
· This is required for any site where public comment is possible
· An approved user agreement is available at http://www.chinfo.navy.mil/socialmedia/user_agreement.doc

☐ **THE PRESENCE MUST BE CLEARLY IDENTIFIED AS "OFFICIAL"**
· Site needs to clearly be identified as an "official" presence
· However, this does not need to appear in the site name

☐ **THE PRESENCE MUST BE UNLOCKED AND OPEN TO THE PUBLIC**
· This primarily applies to Twitter

☐ **ONLY 'OFFICIAL PAGES' ON FACEBOOK CAN BE REGISTERED AND SHOULD BE LABELED AS "ORGANIZATION-GOVERNMENT"**
· The use of Facebook Profile, Community and Group pages for official purposes is not with the government's terms of service agreement with Facebook

☐ **SOCIAL MEDIA PRESENCES IDENTIFYING THE INDIVIDUAL VICE THE COMMAND OR BILLET ARE NOT ACCEPTABLE AS AN "OFFICIAL" PRESENCE WITH THE EXCEPTION OF A NOTABLE FEW (SECNAV, CNO, MCPON).**
· This does not prohibit the use of named accounts by any commander or senior leadership, only the requirement to register the site as "official."

☐ **SUBMIT THE SOCIAL MEDIA PRESENCE FOR APPROVAL AND REGISTRATION TO WWW.NAVY.MIL/SOCIALMEDIA.**

Navy Command Social Media Handbook - Fall 2010

11

Source: U.S. Navy, Office of Navy Information, *Navy Command Social Media Handbook*, Fall 2011, http://www.slideshare.net/USNavySocialMedia/navy-command-social-media-handbook-web.

answers that do not fit the casual tone inherent in social media. By formally distributing the tasks and response functions to those who have the knowledge required to have meaningful online conversations on social media channels, you can decrease maintenance costs (see Section Sixteen), increase trust in those exchanges, and reduce the number of missteps or rounds of interaction it takes before citizens get the "right" response from your agency.

Responsibilities of the organizational units assigned to manage social media applications typically include the following activities:

- Maintaining the actual social media accounts on a daily basis
- Ensuring the use of only approved technologies
- Reviewing and approving content posted on social media channels
- Moderating and monitoring existing content for ongoing accuracy and relevancy
- If necessary, modifying or declining posting of proposed content
- Maintaining and preserving records of content posted on social media sites
- Ensuring that disclaimers are provided and remain relevant
- Reviewing and providing input with regard to terms of service agreements with social networking service providers
- Providing advice on compliance with the existing social media policy
- Assisting with the development and updating of technology-specific guidance documentation and employee conduct policy

Although your social media policy may assign an individual person or unit to lead the charge, the social media workgroup we suggest can provide an effective *sounding board*. Such a group can assist with input and advice representing the entire organization.

BRANDING TO ESTABLISH A "CORPORATE" IDENTITY ACROSS ALL PLATFORMS

Once your agency establishes a brand, it is critical to ensure consistency across all the social media channels you use, particularly if you have individual implementations (that is, separate accounts and account managers for different departments).

With social media, as with any other form of communication, branding is crucial. Carry your off-line brand online, but consider how to optimize it for use in social media. Consistency across all media ensures brand awareness and establishes trust and credibility with your potential audience. The State of Nebraska's *Social Media Guidelines* outlines specifically how state agencies have to brand their social media pages (see Figure 14.2).

Reusing your colors, logos, and slogans on all channels creates a unique corporate identity; it makes clear that even though your agency is using a third-party platform, it is still operating and communicating in an official government context. Consistent branding across your social media outlets demonstrates that users can rely on these outlets as sources of accurate, timely, and relevant information and communications. Figure 14.3 illustrates the consistency in the Federal Communications Commission's branding: all the FCC's social media channels are using the new FCC logo and color scheme where possible.

LISTING OF ALL ACCEPTABLE PLATFORMS

In 2010, the U.S. General Services Administration (GSA) negotiated terms of use agreements with free social networking service providers that guide the use of social media platforms in the U.S. federal government.[5] Likewise, the National Association of State Chief Information Officers (NASCIO) negotiated a similar arrangement in early 2011 for the use of Facebook by states and localities (see Section Two for more information). These negotiated terms of service can serve as guidelines for contractual vehicles or, at a minimum, as guiding documentation for government agencies. Many government agencies use social media policy documents to define specifically which platforms are acceptable and safe to use.

For example, the Strategic Services Division of the Mississippi Department of Information Technology Services outlines in its *Strategic Master Plan for Information Technology 2011–2013* the use of social media for two-way communications.[6]

This master plan document not only lists the appropriate tools but also includes a value statement and examples where relevant. This approach enhances use by informing and educating state agencies with regard to the creative options available to them via social media.

Figure 14.2
Nebraska's Standard for Branding Social Media Pages.

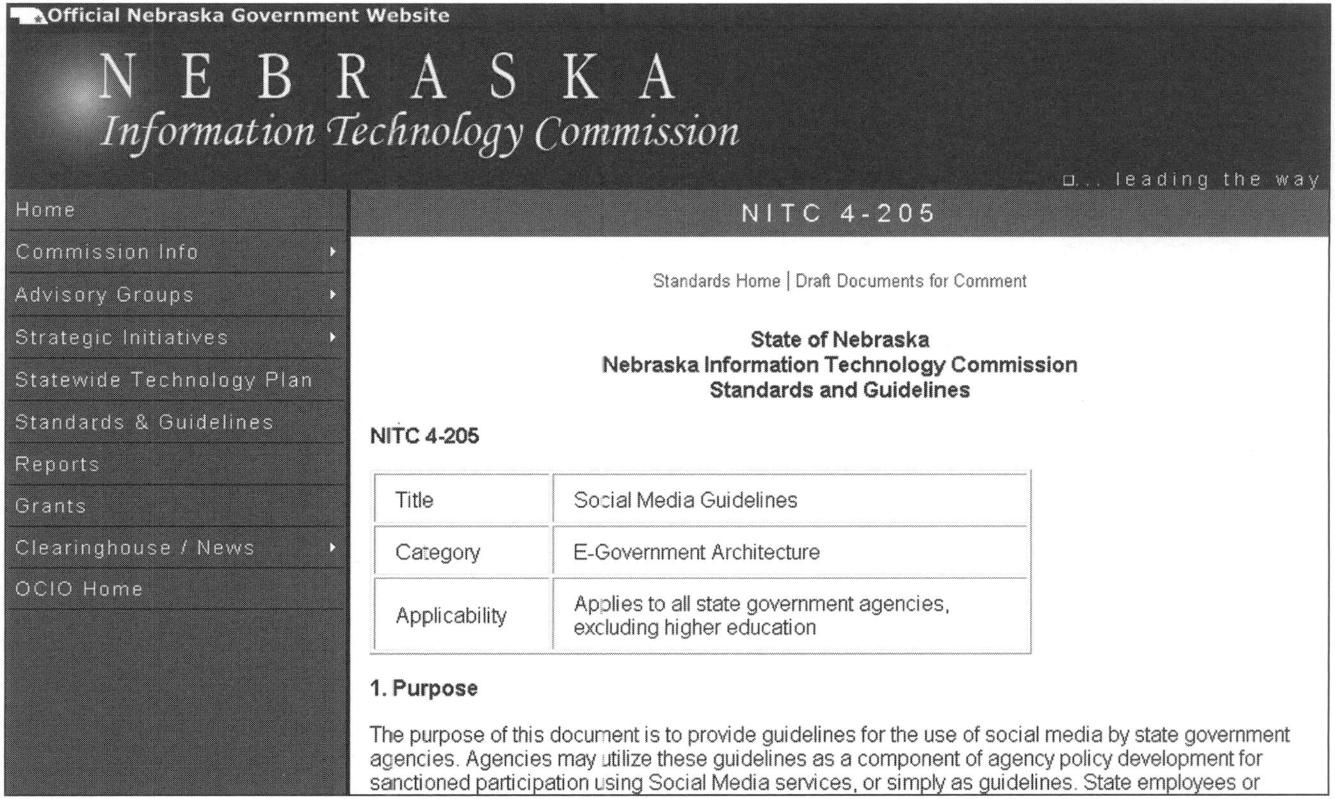

Official Nebraska Government Website

NEBRASKA
Information Technology Commission

🖥 ... leading the way

NITC 4-205

Standards Home | Draft Documents for Comment

Home

Commission Info

Advisory Groups

Strategic Initiatives

Statewide Technology Plan

Standards & Guidelines

Reports

Grants

Clearinghouse / News

OCIO Home

State of Nebraska
Nebraska Information Technology Commission
Standards and Guidelines

NITC 4-205

Title	Social Media Guidelines
Category	E-Government Architecture
Applicability	Applies to all state government agencies, excluding higher education

1. Purpose

The purpose of this document is to provide guidelines for the use of social media by state government agencies. Agencies may utilize these guidelines as a component of agency policy development for sanctioned participation using Social Media services, or simply as guidelines. State employees or

Source: State of Nebraska, Nebraska Information Technology Commission, Standards and Guidelines, *Social Media Guidelines* (NITC 4-205), 2010, http:// www.nitc.ne.gov/standards/4-205.html. Used with the permission of Nebraska Information Technology Commission.

Figure 14.3
FCC Connect's Social Media Branding

Source: U.S. Federal Communications Commission, FCC Connect, [FCC Connect's social media branding], n.d., http://www.fcc.gov/Connect.

THE USE OF SOCIAL MEDIA FOR TWO-WAY COMMUNICATIONS

- State agencies can use **Facebook** to almost instantaneously send out information to other agencies and vendors alike. Creating a Facebook page for a particular division or program can aid in pushing out information about services, programs, procedures, policy, etc. while getting feedback from customers and partners to work together more efficiently.

- **Twitter** can be used to send out information for an upcoming project or program, to notify customers or vendors of pending deadlines, or to post emergency notifications from the proper authorities. Twitter can be used to get information out to a large mass of people whether it is information needed by state agencies, legislators, or citizens.

- The State of Mississippi is already benefitting from the use of **YouTube.** Governor Hailey Barbour uses this application to make his press conferences available to thousands of followers on YouTube. Through the oil spill crisis on the Gulf Coast updates were made available and videos of progress could be seen through the use of this application.

SETTING A CONTENT AND INFORMATION APPROVAL PROCESS

Government documents such as memos or press releases that are made available to the public have traditionally gone through a rigorous vetting process. A knowledge expert or public affairs officer drafts the first version and the legal staff make further changes before the final document is released to the public. Social media are potentially changing this standard process of information production and responsiveness. The new tools allow real-time or near real-time responses to postings on social media channels: a fast back-and-forth conversation between your agency and citizens. Content can be created on the fly instead of through a formal approval process. We therefore suggest thinking about the following questions:

1. How does your agency want to organize the information-vetting process for records created on social media sites?

2. What kind of content do you want to "recycle," or repost, from your website to social media channels? Or is your social media content unique in comparison to your existing website?

3. Whom should you follow on Facebook, Twitter, YouTube, LinkedIn, and the like?

4. Does following and friending mean endorsement of the content provided on third-party platforms?

These are questions you need to answer in your social media strategy and policy. Supplying guidelines on such issues will help to eliminate uncertainties, leading the employees who are responsible for updating your agency's social media accounts toward appropriate decisions.

ENSURING ACCESSIBILITY OF SOCIAL MEDIA CONTENT

Section 508 of the Rehabilitation Act requires that federal agencies' electronic and information technology be accessible to people with disabilities.[7] So your social media policy document should also address the accessibility of your agency's existing communication channels and alternative modes of access. For example, not all social media platforms are accessible for screen readers. A visually impaired audience member might be excluded from participating and engaging through Facebook or Twitter.

A relatively easy solution for adhering to these requirements is to provide the same content on all your communication channels, including print media channels, a website, and social media channels. This is the safe way to ensure that crucial content is accessible through all channels and content is not produced for just one unique channel.

The challenge social media pose is that content is user generated and a government organization is not the sole content provider and producer. Moreover, government has relatively little control over the types of links and media to which citizens are linking. The collaborative networking experience might therefore not be accessible to all people. We recommend always using text equivalents wherever possible to describe multimedia content in order to be as inclusive as possible.

USING PLAIN LANGUAGE ONLINE

Social media applications are a fantastic way to put a human face on the otherwise highly regulated and oftentimes difficult to understand "government speak." Many citizens feel disconnected from their representatives, often citing as a reason the difficulty of understanding the language of government, and text on websites can be misinterpreted or misunderstood. Consider using a more casual and approachable voice in your social media channels. Doing so will help you "go native" within the social media realm, thereby replacing a nameless entity with a friendly voice. Assistance in reducing the risk of being misunderstood and improving people's perception of government accountability is available. The Plain Language Action and Information Network (PLAIN), a group of federal government employees from a diverse set of federal agencies, has prepared the *Federal Plain Language Guidelines*[8] to provide guidance on clear communication, so that users of government websites or social media channels can

- find what they need,
- understand what they find; and
- use what they find to meet their needs.[9]

The guidelines also provide useful tips on how to use plain language techniques when writing for the web. Among them the guide suggests avoiding meaningless formal language:

> Many government websites and letters contain meaningless formal language such as flowery welcome messages and "we hope you get a lot out of our program" messages. Using this type of language wastes space and your users' time. It conveys the impression that you are insincere. Don't waste your users' time. Instead, get directly to the point. Remember, time is money on the web. Keep your important information at the top of a web page. Don't bury it under fluff messages.[10]

KEEPING RECORDS AND COLLECTING PUBLIC INFORMATION

Government agencies in the United States are required to adhere and conform to federal laws, state guidelines, and when applicable, local ordinances concerning the management, archiving, and retention of official records. Although there are no specific guidelines currently mandated in the federal Freedom of Information Act (FOIA), many practitioners predict that it is only a matter of time before government social media archiving is regulated and part of the official public records management Acts.[11]

The requirements of federal e-discovery rules, the federal FOIA, and state-by-state records retention and public records access laws (that is, *sunshine laws*) generally mandate the retention of information based on topic, rather than delivery method. That is to say, content itself, regardless of how it is generated or shared, needs to be evaluated for retention, and whether it takes the form of a document, an e-mail, or a tweet is irrelevant. Some agencies we interviewed have chosen not to archive any materials hosted on a third-party system (a decision that encompasses content on the vast majority of social media platforms) until they receive formal guidelines on the topic. Other agencies have begun taking advantage of archiving tools specific to social media platforms (for example, PageFreezer and Tweettake), or they have created a homegrown process for ensuring accurate records retention for social media channels.

The U.S. National Archives and Records Administration (NARA) provides an interpretation of what constitutes a government record in NARA Bulletin 2011-02 (published October 20, 2010):

> All books, papers, maps, photographs, machine readable materials, or other documentary materials, regardless of physical form or characteristics . . .[12]

This means that content that documents something, independent of the form or format in which the agency generates it, can be interpreted as a government record and should be archived. In the same bulletin NARA provides a checklist that agencies can use to ascertain whether social media content should be considered a public record:

The principles for analyzing, scheduling, and managing records are based on content and are independent of the medium; where and how an agency creates, uses, or stores information does not affect how agencies identify Federal records. When using web 2.0/social media platforms, the following non-exhaustive list of questions may help determine record status:

- Is the information unique and not available anywhere else?
- Does it contain evidence of an agency's policies, business, mission, etc.?
- Is this tool being used in relation to the agency's work?
- Is use of the tool authorized by the agency?
- Is there a business need for the information?

If the answers to any of the above questions are yes, then the content is likely to be a Federal record.

In keeping with these guidelines, White House Director of New Media Macon Phillips points his Twitter followers to the fact that correspondence with him and with the public through his Twitter feed might be subject to the Presidential Records Act and may be archived (see Figure 14.4).

The City of Reno, Nevada, has answered the records retention question with the following statement, drawn from the city's social media policy document:

RECORDS RETENTION

1. Content developers will keep electronic copies of all messages created for and distributed on social media by the City of Reno. Messages posted to the City's newsroom or news blog are archived automatically. Records shall be retained in conformance with the Records Retention Schedules, Policy No. 207.

2. When possible, content developers should avoid creating new material on social media sites. Instead, use existing material from existing

websites or previously published documents to ensure that other forms of the information are retained.

3. When deleting comments or posts, staff should save a screen capture as a jpeg of the content and send it to a public information employee in Public Information for archiving.

4. The City should retain copies of the legal terms and conditions required for creating a social media account.[13]

Figure 14.4
Twitter Account for Macon Phillips, White House Director of New Media.

Macon Phillips (EOP) ⊘
@macon44
An official WH twitter account. Comments & messages received through official WH pages are subject to the PRA and may be archived. Learn more wh.gov/privacy
Washington, DC   http://www.WhiteHouse.gov

Source: M. Phillips, [Twitter account.], n.d., http://twitter.com/macon44.

For now, we encourage those responsible for social media in their agencies to review the record-keeping approaches used within their peer groups and to obtain a thorough review and opinion rendered by the agency's legal counsel as to the best solution to meet their agency's needs.

SETTING A SOCIAL MEDIA COMMENTING POLICY AND ENSURING ONLINE NETIQUETTE

Many government agencies are hesitant to explore social media due to the perception that a Wild West culture prevails on these channels and that they will have little opportunity to manage or influence the conversation. Although it is true that social media operate with much more open standards concerning communication than traditional media do, there are a few common ground rules that you can apply in order to facilitate a healthy and productive exchange of ideas and information via social media.

Rule 1: Develop and Publish a Shared Commenting Policy That Defines the Expectations of Online Discussion

A simple policy stating the conventions of civility in commenting and online discussion is a necessary item for any government social media outlet. This policy defines the agency's expectation of productive discourse and outlines the rules of communication as well as what the agency will not tolerate in discussions (for example, foul language, racism, and so forth). The commenting policy can also define what a user can expect in terms of response time and communication from the agency.

The U.S. Geological Survey's comment policy, displayed in Figure 14.5, provides examples of the types of comments that are inappropriate. The policy first outlines the agency's right to delete specific types of comments and then gives guidance on appropriate conduct. Your agency should state its comment policy in very plain language and post this statement in an easy-to-find location. Your agency can redirect users to the policy on occasion or as needed in order to keep dialogues moving in a constructive direction.

Rule 2: Any Online Communication Should Adhere to the Same Etiquette as Face-to-Face Conversation

You should never use social media as a shield or a barrier. Simply put, do not say anything online that you wouldn't say to a person standing in front of you. Respect your audience's opinions, but use social media to clarify misconceptions and correct false information. Social media dialogues can become a personal task, but avoid incendiary language. Instead, respond to attacks or inflammatory comments in a forgiving manner. You can educate all newcomers to your site about the rules and standards your agency has set and point them to your commenting policy. The State of Utah suggests the following guideline:

> **Conversational:** Talk to your readers like you would talk to people in professional situations. Avoid overly "composed" language. Bring in your own personality and say what is on your mind. Consider content that is open-ended and invites response. Encourage comments. Broaden the conversation by citing others who are commenting about the same topic and allowing your content to be shared or syndicated.[14]

Figure 14.5
The USGS's Comment Policy.

U.S. Geological Survey (USGS) ▸ Comment Policy

🖒 Like

Government Organization · Reston, Virginia

We welcome your comments and hope that our conversations here will be polite. You are responsible for the content of your comments.

We reserve the ability to delete any of the following:

- violent, obscene, profane, hateful, or racist comments
- comments that threaten or harm the reputation of any person or organization
- advertisements or solicitations of any kind
- comments that suggest or encourage illegal activity
- off-topic posts or repetitive posts that are copied and pasted
- personal information including, but not limited to, email addresses, telephone numbers, mailing addresses, or identification numbers
- comments which may cause public panic or falsely cite the deployment of emergency services (e.g., "major earthquake to strike Los Angeles in next 24 hours!").

In short: be nice, be mature, and add to the discussion. If you have any questions or comments about this policy, please email us.

Note: If we do delete comments from this page, or associated USGS profiles, for violating our Comment Policy above, we will not collect any personal information related to the comment. We will only collect the comment itself. If we delete a comment, we will remove any personal information contained within that comment to the best of our ability, before capturing it.

Source: U.S. Geological Survey, "Comment Policy," n.d., https://www.facebook.com/USGeologicalSurvey?sk=app_190322544333196.

In addition you can try to rephrase their questions, ask for clarification, repeat the questions in your own words, and try to understand and then respond in an appropriate manner. The ultimate goal is to make your audience members feel good about their engagement with government. The upside is that you make your audience look good and provide an overall positive experience that makes people want to come back.

At times citizens get very upset, especially when they feel mistreated and misunderstood by government. If discussions or comments are overheating and are disrespectful, try responding privately. Point out major mistakes politely, and avoid embarrassing anyone in public.

Rule 3: Accept and Respond Positively to Differing Points of View

For most, if not all, government organizations, the commenting aspect of social media becomes an issue of free speech. Is Facebook a public forum? And if so, what level of control does an organization have over the comments made? Many government agencies regard social media outlets as similar to public meetings. They define the outlets as *limited public forums*, in which citizens have a right to speak and be heard within defined guidelines of civility.

As mentioned previously, agencies should develop and post a commenting policy that defines acceptable behavior and conventions of discourse. However, be prepared for the legitimate and courteous criticism your audience may provide. Regardless of the legal or policy aspects of social media as communication channels, trust and open dialogue are essential to their ongoing value as tools for government agencies.

In 2011, New York State Senator Joseph Robach's office experienced this first-hand when staff pulled from the senator's Facebook page comments they considered unflattering. A local newspaper reported the story:

> When some of state Sen. Joseph Robach's constituents were upset with his vote against gay marriage, they took to his Facebook page to register their complaints. A short time later, their comments were removed. Actually, all comments from other Facebook users, regardless of the topic, were removed from Robach's page.[15]

This action, taken without notice or explanation, left the senator's constituency feeling disrespected and with concerns that the incident violated their freedom of speech. As soon as you start to use social media for your agency, you will notice that citizens want to comment and to use these additional channels not only as a means to get directly in touch with government but also as platforms for discussions with like-minded others. These public discussions might not shine a positive light on your agency, but unless they violate your stated commenting policy, you should not ever delete them. Refute inaccuracies in a positive tone, but welcome debate and discussion. Even though you may have the technical ability and the legal right to remove comments, doing so will undermine the agency's online credibility and you will lose your audience (and the immediate impact value of the channel).

Rule 4: Respect Your Audience

Although citizen conduct is important, it is equally important to think about how you can protect your audience's privacy. Think about *what* you as a government authority share from your audience's messages and also *how* you share it via your agency's outlets. Even when citizens are oversharing, seek their permission to share information they give you, unless they themselves have posted the information in a forum visible to others as well as to you.

Few citizens want to hear from their government as much as their government would like to communicate with them. Most don't have the time to read all of your agency's information, and some do not have sufficient bandwidth to entertain a heavy flow of information. Instead, think strategically about when most users might be reading their social media newsfeeds. Try a variety of schedules, such as early morning, during lunch breaks, and at night.

Consider the value of information before you post it. Does it pertain to a matter that clearly relates to your agency? How recent was your previous posting? Will the content further the mission or is it simply fluff? You don't want to over-engage and thereby disengage your audience. Given the amount of information and number of news outlets available today, social media audiences have the prerogative and inclination to be fickle about the resources they maintain. Once you lose them, it may be very difficult to gain them back. Be proactive, and consider the value of your messages from the recipient's perspective before you send them.

The social media guidelines of the Nebraska Information Technology Commission summarize suggestions for online conduct in the form of a best practices list:

2.9   Best Practices. Suggestions on how best to use and maintain social networking at work:

    2.9.1 Ensure that your agency sanctions official participation and representation on Social Media sites. Stick to your area of

(continued)

expertise and provide unique, individual perspectives on what is going on at the State and in other larger contexts. All statements must be true and not misleading, and all claims must be substantiated and approved.

2.9.2 Post meaningful, respectful comments, no spam, and no remarks that are off-topic or offensive. When disagreeing with others' opinions, keep it appropriate and polite.

2.9.3 Pause and think before posting. Reply to comments in a timely manner when a response is appropriate unless you have posted a disclaimer that this is not official two-way communication.

2.9.4 Be smart about protecting yourself, your privacy, your agency, and any restricted, confidential, or sensitive information. What is published is widely accessible, not easily retractable, and will be around for a long time (even if you remove it), so consider the content carefully. Respect proprietary information, content, and confidentiality.

2.9.5 If you are under a generic name (see Section 2.6 above) consider using some form of tagging so staff and users can find out who this is.

2.9.6 Email or login names should lead the user back to a "state id," such as an official state email address or make a user name that indicates you are a state employee.[16]

Summary Review

- Determine who will be responsible for your social media efforts. Will it rest with a single agency, or will it be distributed across multiple employees or departments?

- Be sure to identify a consistent branding for all of your social media channels. Image, color scheme, tone, and so forth should all be the same across each platform.

- Early on, establish a process to review content and determine which social media platform(s) are acceptable.

- Be sure to use plain language in your social media channels in order to establish accessibility and interest.

- Although records retention laws regarding social media are still somewhat vague, you can use technology archiving services and best practices for the retention of other documentation as a general process for retaining social media records.

- These common ground rules about making comments should assist you in developing long-term value:

    Develop and publish a shared comment policy that defines the expectations for online discussion.

    Make it clear that any online communication should adhere to the same etiquette as face-to-face conversation.

    Accept and respond positively to differing points of view.

    Respect your audience.

Employee Social Media Use

Personal Versus Professional

So far this guide has been focused on the tools, concepts, and processes of using social media as part of an agency's formal communication strategy, driving two-way communication between agency and audience. But these new forms of communication can also have tremendous impact on the employees of government agencies as individuals. As we discussed in earlier sections, social media evolved out of common interests and activities, and many government employees are using social media for their private interactions with friends or other professionals. Social media evolved organically as a combination of technology and community, not as work tools. Therefore it is inevitable that many employees who may (or may not) be tasked with managing an agency's social media presence may also use social media for personal reasons. How do government agencies advocate and practice the use of social media for constituent interaction while at the same time managing the personal use of social media by agency employees? In addition, how can government provide guidance that keeps employees safe from unintended lapses on social networking platforms that might by extension affect government as an employer?

As mentioned in earlier sections, social media represent a major shift in our ability to communicate with stakeholders and our varied audiences. Using social media enables us to personalize communication and reach multiple audiences beyond our own sphere of direct communication, with little effort or expense. Yet it also requires us to set aside our typical bureaucratic language and adopt a friendlier, conversational tone.[1]

Social media require that agencies be accepting of a new work culture that may not sit well with traditional modes of productivity. They require an easy comfort with self-managed technology. Their use frequently happens outside the cubicle and the typical workday hours. Success at this implementation requires us to take our cues from the new norms of communication inherent in social media and driven by the social media uses of citizens. Some have described government use of social media as a hybrid of a public forum and casual water-cooler conversation: an informal yet productive exchange of ideas in the hallways. Typically this approach requires an increase in trust that individual employees will represent the agency's goals and objectives appropriately through social media channels. To be sure, this trust also requires each individual to appropriately and respectfully represent the agency. Overall, asking employees to accept some general guidance and to have a dose of common sense appears to be the most common story of social media implementation.

As discussed in Section Twelve, an organization's social media strategy provides the guidance and underlying value statement for the use of social media in ways specific to an agency's mission. Many social media policies dictate which social media tools should and should not be used as part of an agency's online presence. The social media policy should remain an organizational resource, providing overarching guidance as to how social media can and should be integrated into the agency's overall communications strategy and its mission.

Agencies cannot always control or dictate the way constituencies will use social media platforms and tools. Policies need to set boundaries focused on the agency's needs, yet they must have the flexibility to adapt to the way the platforms are changing and any new ways in which audiences are using those platforms. Flexibility and adaptability will ensure greater longevity for any personal use guidance in the policies.

Because social media make up such a new phenomenon, many of the policies we reviewed also blended in directives for employee behavior related to personal use of social media. However, we believe that a strong distinction should be drawn between agency guidelines and employee personal behavior. The social media policy should remain focused purely on the objectives, rules, and guidelines for using social media as a sanctioned component of achieving the agency mission.

THE BLURRING OF LINES

Given the person-centric focus of social media, how can an employee draw the distinction between corporate and personal use? And is it truly a good thing to draw such a drastic distinction? The most obvious (albeit sometimes the most difficult to maintain) solution is to create a solid division between personal and professional. Under this approach, employees who manage a social media presence strictly for personal reasons do not mention their employment in a profile. They do not join groups or comment on topics relative to their specific agency. They maintain a profile focused on their personal interests or a generic focus on their industry.

But what happens when an employee meets colleagues face-to-face at a conference and wants to maintain a professional online relationship? And how does a professional demonstrate his or her industry expertise when responding to a topical blog? Job titles open doors, even in the online world. Gathering and participating in a community and joining in online discussions can lead to informal learning opportunities and industry connections with peers in similar positions.

These experiences can make an employee a more valuable organizational asset as well. The organic blending of personal and professional, managed properly, can be beneficial to the employee and the employer. When an employee creates a social media presence, it expands the boundaries of the organization. It opens new channels of information from peers, constituents, and other organizations. It can lead to informal professional development and the strengthening of relevant sounding boards for new ideas. Forging such channels can enable access to innovative information from new (and affordable) sources.

Many professionals participate in LinkedIn, feeling that it offers a more business-focused and safe social media environment than other platforms do. LinkedIn is an excellent tool for maintaining an exclusively professional social media presence. It enables users to create professional, résumé-type profiles and communicate with colleagues, join professional groups, and post work-related content in a professional framework designed within a social framework. Government organizations are finding creative ways to capitalize on their indirect presence on social networks through their employees by encouraging those individuals to tell the organization's "story" in the individual's own words and across his or her own networks. In August of 2011, the U.S. Navy published a presentation encouraging Navy personnel to consider using LinkedIn as a way to "tell the Navy story and increase awareness of what the Navy does," even if they are not looking for a job.[2]

SETTING ACCEPTABLE USE POLICIES

Many agencies already have in place policies that govern the use of agency-owned assets for personal use. We reviewed several *acceptable use* policies that included explicit do's and don'ts regarding desktop phones (for example, no personal long-distance calls), computers (for example, no online gambling or political activity), and other technologies. Many agencies also address the personal use of social media on agency-owned computers and other devices and while employees are on the clock. Some governments now extend their acceptable use policies to the use of social media on behalf of government. The State of Michigan provides explicit employee instructions for using the state web-

> Social Media Site Account Administrators must:
>
> Be responsible for creating, maintaining and monitoring content on respective social media sites, engaging with users, and removing content that violates SOM web and social media standards.
>
> Avoid replicating content. Content that is posted outside SOM portal sites should refer to or identify and link back to the original content.
>
> Refrain from posting content that violates city, state, or federal laws and regulations.
>
> Always respond to constituent inquiries and postings using the official State-approved account for the respective agencies. Do not use non-State (personal) accounts to respond to inquiries or postings.
>
> Respond to all inquiries or comments and post within one (1) business day. All replies should use professional conversational language that encourages comments and engages follow-up conversation.
>
> Not comment on or post anything related to legal matters or litigation without appropriate approval.
>
> Not use the State's name or graphical representation (logos) to endorse any view, product, private business, cause or political candidate.
>
> Not represent personal opinions as State-endorsed views or policies.
>
> Adhere to existing policy when the State Emergency Operations Center or state's Joint Information Center is activated. All content related to the emergency will be disseminated through accounts maintained by the Emergency Management and Homeland Security Division of the Michigan State Police or designated lead department.[3]

site, Michigan.gov, including the following guidance on acceptable use of social media tools and channels.

Although it is possible to include mandates regarding social media in such concrete guidelines, the evolving nature of social media and their networks requires constant monitoring and responsiveness from government to stay on top of the newest developments. As we've mentioned earlier, social media are not simply about technology, so notions about using them don't fit easily into categories of good or bad. Changing tools, the rapid advancement of smart-phone use, and the ever-increasing blurring of the distinctions between personal and professional life will make any heavy-handed approach intended to "control" social media use difficult to administer. At this point, because social media are still relatively new phenomena in the public sector, many agencies do not yet have formal policies to govern acceptable corporate and personal uses of the tools. Some rely on unwritten guidelines, corporate culture, or other such intangible controls to govern its use. Asking employees to seek formal permission to use social media is also a thorny issue in that it can be argued that any sort of directive policy can stretch too far into an employee's individual rights outside the workplace.

> The County acknowledges employee rights to privacy and free speech that may protect on-line activity conducted on personal social networks. However, what is published on such personal sites should not be attributed to or reference the County and should not appear to be endorsed by or originated from the County. Employees that choose to list their work affiliation or reference their employment with the County in any way on a social network should regard all communication on that network as if it were a professional network.
>
> On-line lives are ultimately linked, whether or not employees choose to mention the County on personal on-line networks. County employees engaging in social media networks must at all times be conscious and respectful of the fact that their words and actions are representative of the County, regardless of when, where and how the content was posted.[4]

A more effective solution is to incorporate language regarding social media into a code of conduct or personnel manual that more generally describes the agency's expectations of professionalism and conduct on the part of its employees. An excerpt from the employee handbook for Roanoke County, Virginia, illustrates how personal social media use and expectations of employee conduct might be linked.

A general, broad approach will suffice for the majority of employees, and agencies can deal with exceptions on a more specific, case-by-case basis. Providing guidance and expectations, rather than implementing controls, will endow the agency's policies with greater effectiveness.

USING DISCLAIMERS AND IDS ON PERSONAL SOCIAL MEDIA ACCOUNTS

Additionally, we came across many government employees who used a disclaimer of sorts on their personal social media accounts. These disclaimers served to draw a distinction between their personal, yet informed, opinions and the formal standpoints of their employers. Figures 15.1, 15.2, and 15.3 offer examples of such disclaimers from three individuals. We also asked each individual for the reasoning behind his or her disclaimer.

KRISTY FIFELSKI, WEB MANAGER FOR RENO, NEVADA

The reason I included the disclaimer is because it's good practice as I identified my employer in my profile. Also, it's a part of our formal social media policy: If an employee can easily be identified with, or identifies themselves as, a City of Reno employee on their blog or other social media profile, they should make it clear to their readers that the views expressed in their blog entries do not necessarily reflect the City's views. To help reduce the potential for confusion, the following notice—or something similar—should be put in a reasonably prominent place on their site: "The views expressed on this blog are mine alone and do not necessarily reflect the views of my employer, the City of Reno."

JANET CLAGGETT, CHIEF INFORMATION OFFICER FOR RICHLAND COUNTY, SOUTH CAROLINA

The disclaimer was intended to provide dual protection. On the one side, I wanted to protect my employer from being held responsible for anything I might tweet. Even though it was never my intention to tweet anything that would offend someone, I am realistic enough to recognize that being offended is in the eye of the beholder. On the other side, I wanted to protect myself, in an effort to give myself the freedom to explore social media without feeling like my hands were excessively tied.

About

This website is the personal blog of Bill Schrier, Chief Technology Officer for the City of Seattle, used to express personal opinion. Comments on any blog entry are welcome, but will be moderated. The opinions expressed on this site and in the blog are solely those of Bill Schrier and do not necessarily reflect the official opinions of the elected officials or residents of the City of Seattle.

The focus of this blog is the intersection of technology and government, and specifically how technology influences Seattle's government, but also how governments use technology on behalf of their residents, citizens, and visitors.

The official website of the City of Seattle is www.seattle.gov , and the official website for the City's Department of Information Technology, which Bill directs, is www.seattle.gov/doit . Official City of Seattle blogs are on

Source: B. Schrier. Used with the permission of Bill Schrier.

BILL SCHRIER, CHIEF INFORMATION OFFICER, SEATTLE, WASHINGTON

The wording was a standard disclaimer which, for some years, we used with e-mail at the City of Seattle.

More importantly, I am a public figure at the City government, working directly for an elected Mayor. My blog site is not hosted by the City, but I did post my name and title on the blog. It is important that readers understand I don't write "officially" in my official capacity working for City government. Only the Mayor and other elected officials can make City policy.

I've been challenged by certain folks who say I should remove my title and affiliation completely from the blog. However, it is relatively easy to Bing search and find my "day job." So, rather than have people think that I may or may not represent the Mayor in my writing, I add the disclaimer. Also, I think it important that people know a little bit about my background and experience from which the blog observations spring.

City Engineer/Assistant Director of Public Works of a city in Illinois

Tapping into the Collective Intelligence

Social media tools have been most beneficial to me as a way of easily connecting with other professionals working in or for government. When I was employed by a rural community some years ago, I had few opportunities to find and speak with others in my field who were not coworkers. And even though this situation prevented me from learning valuable lessons from others facing similar everyday challenges, it was particularly devastating during those times when those of us in the public works department were faced with unusual problems. Thinking back to some of those times, I know that the ability to tap into social media would have made a significant difference in how well we handled those issues.

One example I often think of involved a problem we had with our water treatment plant. A few months after starting up the new plant, we began receiving complaints of meat staying red after cooking. At first we were hesitant to accept that it was due to the city's water; after all, people were always blaming the water for causing all sorts of things. Once we even had a guy show up at the water billing counter complaining that the city's water was causing him problems with his urine. When it was suggested that perhaps there was some other cause, he plopped a large jar of his urine on the counter, as if showing a sample of the foul liquid was proof enough. So after going through these types of experiences, it's probably not surprising that we had become skeptical. But one day I tried cooking a roast myself and realized the problem probably did have something to do with the water.

Now, the water operators I worked with were far from inexperienced. We also had a water chemist from a local industry working with us at the plant on a regular basis who was very knowledgeable. But not one of us had ever heard of water preventing meat from turning brown when cooked. I tried searching on the Internet for information, but because this happened in the early 1990s, there was little information to be found. Only after weeks of wondering and researching on our own did I think to call a meat department at a university in the Midwest. Fortunately, one of the professors there was able to give us an important clue—he said the only things he could think of that made meat stay red were nitrates or nitrites. He explained that's why hot dogs don't turn brown when cooked—they have nitrates or nitrites. And once we shared this with our chemist, he knew exactly what had happened. A growth had taken hold in our system and was producing nitrates or nitrites as a waste product. The simple fix was to overchlorinate the water until the growth died. Fortunately, at the levels of nitrates and nitrites we had, there was no health risk to the public.

If that had been the only outcome of that incident, it would not have been so bad. But while we were trying to find the solution, the local newspaper got hold of the story and blew the whole thing out of proportion, scaring people into thinking they could never drink the water. I am sure that still today in that community, people are unnecessarily buying bottled water due to those newspaper articles. Things got almost to the point where we would have had to turn off the water plant.

Several months after the dust settled on that problem, we read in an industry magazine an article about a similar problem in a community where a major chicken distributor was located. We contacted the person who solved that community's problem, and he eventually visited us so we could share information about these experiences.

The whole episode played out over about eight months, but had this happened today, we would have been able to take advantage of social media to investigate and solve our problem—not only by reaching out to our customers to more quickly learn the details of what they were experiencing, but also by taking advantage of the collective knowledge of our profession through posting our problem on social media sites. We would likely have identified and solved the problem within days.

Today when I have a question about how best to solve a problem, I often put up a post on sites like Twitter or LinkedIn. Almost always, another professional answers within hours with a suggested solution. And many times that professional works in another country. If I don't find an answer I can use by posting on these sites, I can reach out directly through Skype to talk to others working in my industry whom I have met through interacting on social media sites.

In addition, for the past five years I have been directly exploring how others employed in public works, engineering, and government can best use social media and 3D immersive technology to enhance their work. I have cofounded MuniGov 2.0, an online group for those working to implement social media and 3D technology in local government, I manage a public works–related website, and I publish *Grid Works*, an online magazine reporting on engineering and government-related uses of 3D immersive technology.

So for me, social media tools are all about meeting and communicating with others. They are a pathway for tapping into an international collective intelligence within my profession. They're a direct route to educational opportunities that can be delivered to my desk. They're a tool through which I can offer my own experiences to others. And they have significantly changed the way I research and solve problems.

Although the legality of such informal disclaimers and the protection offered by them are yet to be fully tested, the general community consensus is that "it can't hurt" to have one. A disclaimer will not excuse blatant violations of an employee code of conduct, but it will strengthen the distinction between an individual's work role and personal life.

Summary Review

- Both agencies and employees must recognize the fact that social media blur the lines between corporate and personal use, and they must therefore adjust accordingly.

- Acceptable use policies work best for social media use when they encourage employees to use good judgment and common sense, rather than trying to identify all the do's and don'ts of social media.

- Employees who use social media on a personal basis should consider adding a disclaimer to their personal accounts to clarify that the views they express on these accounts do not necessarily reflect the views of their employer.

Implementation

As your agency develops its social media strategy and tactics, defines its social media policy, and sets parameters for employees' professional and personal uses of social media, it should also be considering the best ways to implement these decisions. In this section we suggest several approaches that can lead to successful implementation: developing a workgroup of stakeholders, identifying ongoing social media maintenance costs and looking for ways to reduce this burden, and devising controlled experiments in communication and interaction that require the setting of goals and the measurement of success.

DEVELOPING A WORKGROUP

As we have discussed in earlier sections, using social media in government is not about technology; it is about adopting a cultural change that puts your constituents in closer communication and collaboration with their governing body. There is no one person or department that can successfully implement a social media strategy alone. In many of the agencies where we conducted our interviews, early successes were often the work of individuals across the organization who were excited by social media and understood both their uses and their potential. Oftentimes, this loose affiliation of early adopters did not conform to traditional organizational roles.

For long-term strategy development, we recommend identifying a core group of users focused on identifying, championing, and implementing the social media strategies and policies of your organization. Following are some of the areas that we suggest should be represented in the membership of an implementation workgroup.

Administration The office of your agency's chief administrative officer is a crucial component of a social media workgroup. Participation may range from

141

simply giving permission to move forward with the concepts all the way to providing full leadership and advocacy across the organization. The senior administrative official is ultimately responsible for all the organization's decisions and has to answer to legislators and the public. Administrative participation (regardless of the level) is crucial for the longevity of any social media program. If your administration does not participate directly in the workgroup, provide regular progress updates to ensure continued executive support.

Legal Counsel   Social media by their very nature can move an organization into a new realm of interaction with the public, and this can translate into concerns regarding privacy, e-discovery, freedom of information, public forums, intellectual property, and liability. Cultivating an ally in your legal counsel to address these issues as part of agency's larger social media strategy gives you another crucial member of the workgroup. The legal aspects of social media are very particular—each technology channel you use will likely have its own inherent concerns that need to be addressed, and each organization's counsel will have a particular perspective on the issues surrounding such use. Involving your counsel from the beginning will mitigate many of the potential pitfalls.

Information Technology   Although social media are not simply about technology, they do rely heavily on technology to function. Even though most social media applications do not require an on-premises technology infrastructure or support staff, these applications do pose potential headaches for a technology department in the areas of security, licensing, training, and user support. Additionally, social media require a cultural change in traditional technology departments in that social media rely on infrastructure that is not under internal control. As technology leaders perform a balancing act between security and business value, it is imperative that they understand the big picture of their agency's social media implementation from its inception, so that they can provide feedback and input early on in the process.

Public Information and Marketing   Much of the value of social media from a public information perspective lies in the new ways it offers for sharing information that already exists. The public information officer can be a tremendous resource and advocate for social media tools because he or she is always focused on crafting the message and finding memorable ways to engage the population.

If you are also fortunate enough to have access to some talented design people, they can help you maintain consistent branding across your agency's social media channels.

Human Resources and Workforce Development   The Millennials entering the workforce today have expectations different from those of previous generations. To them, technology is inherent in their daily lives. They expect easy access and usability in the workplace as well. Recruiting methods, evaluation tactics, and performance measurements are all subject to change as they are adapted to a shifting work culture. By involving your agency's human resource department, you can explore and exploit social media as an avenue for recruitment and internal communication to help keep pace with the evolving workplace.

Economic Development and Tourism   If a picture is worth a thousand words, how much value would you place on a mashup that puts a picture in context with tagging, feedback, and semantic links to related resources? If your agency has an economic development group, it will focus on one thing—making the local area the most appealing option for people looking to spend their money or to settle down. A relocating business, a family looking to vacation in a new spot, and even just a professional group looking for the best venue to hold its next annual conference can all lead to revenue for your locality. The development group spends big money and big time to make the appeal of the local area distinct from the appeal of a sea of similar sites across the region, the state, the country, or even the world. Social media offer the development group a creative and dynamic new potential to present the appeal of the local jurisdiction's demographics, attractions, and capabilities. This group should be represented in your workgroup.

Direct Citizen Service Business Units   It is also wise to include one or two of the business units that are in direct, daily contact with your agency's constituents. Local libraries, parks and recreation departments, youth commissions, community liaisons, and the like serve all the demographics of your community, and they generally know how its citizens want to receive and share information. Many libraries and park systems are well versed in the use of social media to get the message out about their news and events. These agencies also typically have a practical understanding of marketing honed from years of working directly with the population, so they probably already "get" social media.

Any of these organizations will likely be an enthusiastic and valuable addition to your workgroup mix. Ultimately, social media can become everyone's responsibility. Many agencies recognize that individuals at any level or station in an organization can become *social media ambassadors* for the agency's mission and strategy. Once you start looking across your organization, you may find other willing participants who are already familiar with the tools and concepts. You may also want to consider direct participation from your community on the information and social media channels they would prefer. Gather as much information as you can and include as many sources as is logistically possible—the more inclusive you can be at the beginning, the better your workgroup's chances are for long-term success. The workgroup will help you start the initiative, but when the process matures, the use of social media will proliferate across the organization and the social media policy will provide guidance and set expectations.

Recognizing (and Minimizing) Costs

Although social media do not typically require significant capital costs, they do require an ongoing maintenance cost, often in the form of staff time. Social media require ongoing care and feeding in order to be most effective. Their personalized approach to information delivery means that these tools require human interaction. The need to monitor social media channels, ensure timely information distribution, and make responses, follow-ups, and regular updates means that someone is going to be responsible and accountable for an agency's efforts. Many agencies use automation tools such as RSS to eliminate duplication of effort. This enables agencies to post information in one location and have it automatically distributed to other content outlets.

With regard to social media staffing, some agencies, particularly in larger organizations, pursue a single point of responsibility for all social content. However, many organizations have managed to avoid this personnel cost by distributing the workload among several positions across the organization. This latter approach lends itself well to the cultural transformation brought about by social media by fostering the notion that rather than continuing the traditionally structured workflow around distributing information, all employees can be ambassadors for the organization.

As social media continue to rise in use within government, agencies may feel a resources strain as they try to maintain a presence on all channels. However, we believe there may come a tipping point where social media use in government becomes ubiquitous and surpasses the use of traditional media formats, at which time a more formal reorganization of communication roles can occur. Using automation tools, distributing content responsibility (along with guidance), and reducing reliance on traditional outlets will enable agencies to weather the change in communication strategy.

Using Controlled Experiments

We caution against deploying social media initiatives simply because your agency can. Taking a measured, successful approach to the use of social media in government begins, like all communication plans, with a thorough understanding of specific goals. Although the tools described in this field guide are powerful and easy to use, they are simply a means to an end. Deploying the tools without a surrounding plan will lead to only a brief spark rather than a lasting impact. Design the tool set and the deployment with the goal in mind. What is your agency attempting to do? Educate? Communicate? Seek input? Goals should be attainable and, more important, measurable. Consider documenting your goals in a form that makes them specific. Here's an example:

> **Goal:** To educate the citizens of the Woodlands neighborhood about the pros and cons of a new skateboard ramp and gather their input prior to the formal city council vote on August 1.

The goal is specific—it outlines the audience, the time frame, and the focus. Now you can take this goal and determine whether and how social media can assist in achieving it. Start with your audience. What do you know about your audience? Who are they? How do they get their information? Would they be accessible via social media? How could you use traditional methods to drive social media participation?

Once you have evaluated your audience, you can proceed with selecting a tool (or multiple tools) that you believe will have the most effective reach for your target market and goal. As we mentioned, the tools themselves are relatively easy to implement and generally have a low cost of entry (particularly compared to traditional technology tools). This low cost of entry and relative ease of use enables experimentation without fear of poor stewardship.

Next, if you are specifically trying to measure the success of the social media aspects of your goal, define your success at a granular level. How will you determine if the campaign was worth the effort? Choose measurements specific to social media:

Success measure: We receive 100 comments on the Facebook poll regarding the skate park.

Success measure: Blog participation on the topic increases by 15 percent or the @woodlandsskatepark Twitter account attracts 200 followers.

These experiments should not become a time and resource hog. To reduce your time overhead, consider recycling content from other areas to jump-start your experimentation. Try using content developed for other outlets, such as meeting minutes, news releases, event listings, and the like, to get things rolling. But be aware that this same content, in this new forum, will (it is to be hoped) generate dialogue and feedback.

There is no one-size-fits-all approach to a social media deployment. Each initiative can (and should) be customized to reach a defined segment of your constituency. Deploying social media is not the answer to *all* communication or service delivery issues faced by the public sector. But it is certainly the one to watch—social media are evolving and improving with each new tool and each new trend they foster. With social media come new potential, new benefits, new issues, and new requirements. In order to be effective, focus social media use on an audience that already exists for your topic or issue. Also be aware that social media might not replace a traditional website or print communications or the televised public service announcements focused on your constituents.

PART FOUR

Where Do We Go from Here?

This is no longer a gimmick. This is how the American people want to receive their news and want to hear from us.

—Nick Schaper, when he was director of new media for
House Minority Leader John Boehner[1]

As evident from the previous sections, social media, and particularly their use within government, continue to evolve at a rapid pace. The concepts have established a strong foothold, but the actual delivery methods are still fluctuating and growing to meet the needs of users and their audience.

In Part Two, we discussed the tools available and most frequently employed today. In Part Three, we provided guidance on how to successfully put those tools into practice. But this book would be incomplete without a look ahead to what is coming next. Part Four offers a summary of some of the emerging technologies and tools being tested in the public sector. These tools have had limited exposure and success to date. But as their adoption and popularity continue to grow, we feel that they warrant at least an introductory glance.

The Future of Social Media in the Public Sector

Predictions on how social media will evolve over time are difficult to make because the direction of this evolution is set mostly by the innovative behavior of service providers but also more and more by the needs and inventions stemming from the innovative social media behavior of citizens. One survey found that in 2011, 65 percent of all adult Americans were using social networking sites, such as Facebook or LinkedIn, up from 8 percent in 2005.[1] This growing popularity of social networking sites is a vital reason for government agencies to start offering services and information through social networking sites.

Going forward, we believe that the use of social media in government will go beyond basic Facebook profiles, tweets, and blog posts that merely accompany information available through traditional media outlets, websites, or e-mail lists. Instead, the use of social media in government will become more engaging and will focus on actual knowledge transfer and innovation creation by citizens. In this final section we'll provide a glimpse into the use of some innovative platforms that are just now making their way into government.

OPEN INNOVATION PLATFORMS FOR IDEA CROWDSOURCING

Social media tools such as blogs, Twitter, and Facebook are great channels for citizens to use to provide their insights on the issues and plans of government. Unfortunately, today's standard social networking services do not have the capability to automatically extract and collate new knowledge or ideas from content that citizens are submitting through these existing commenting channels. In some cases the sheer volume of comments makes proper analysis

149

very difficult. The challenge is to extract new ideas or valuable insights from the influx of comments in a productive and efficient way. Moreover, not all information that a government needs in order to innovate is always readily available.[2]

Open innovation platforms are designed to fill this gap. Using a crowdsourcing approach on one of these platforms, government agencies can issue an open call to a large, usually broadly defined group of people (citizens in general, potential contractors or industry representatives, citizen programmers, and so forth), so that many different people can contribute to the solution of a complex task. The platform then helps the agency to direct and coordinate the input from the group of citizens (or application developers, knowledge matter experts, companies, and so forth)—input that would typically be uncategorized, unstructured, and overwhelming on social media channels. These crowdsourcing mechanisms are useful for issues where expert knowledge might not be available or is too expensive to access. They also help to improve the participation and engagement of citizens. Crowdsourcing provides a platform through which governments can engage citizens directly in the decision-making process.[3]

Virtually any government topic can be crowdsourced, meaning that agencies can post an issue in the form of a *challenge* and ask for the submission of solutions. The focus is on innovation, creativity, and the generation of new ideas from stakeholders and subject matter experts. The agency will select the best solution or set of solutions, and the people who submitted these solutions are often compensated in some way. This approach is more cost-effective than the traditional requests for proposals, which are often time-consuming and have specific design criteria and a specific kind of solution in mind. A challenge opens the conversation and allows the *crowd* to come up with the solution, often without rigid requirement constraints.

The U.S. General Services Administration (GSA) has created a website tool called Challenge.gov that takes on the task of collecting public feedback on a specific issue. As the website says, "Challenge.gov is a place where the public and government can solve problems together" (Figure 17.1). The platform allows participating agencies to post their own challenges and invite the submission of ideas and solutions from citizens. "Challenges can range from fairly simple (idea suggestions or the creation of logos, videos, digital games, and mobile applications)

Figure 17.1
Challenge.gov.

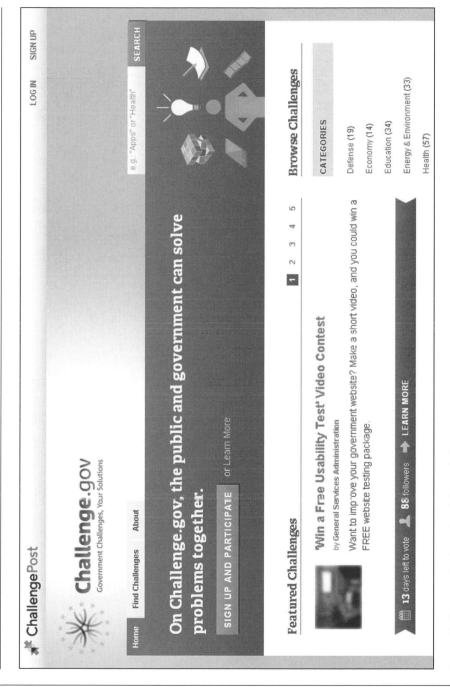

Source: Challenge.gov, [Web page], n.d., http://challenge.gov.

Figure 17.2
Challenge.gov Participation Process.

Government posts   Citizens share   Talented people find
challenges.   with their friends.   solutions to the problem.

Source: Copyright © 2012 by Ines Mergel and Bill Greeves.

to proofs of concept, designs, or finished products that solve the grand challenges of the 21st century" (Figure 17.2).[4]

Local governments are also using open innovation platforms in a similar fashion. New York City's NYC Simplicity has been used to generate cost-saving ideas from employees (Figure 17.3). The City of Mesa, Arizona's iMesa program is a response to the economic downturn, designed to collect citizens' ideas to save money. Harford County, Maryland's innovation portal also solicits ideas from constituents in order to stimulate new ideas and innovation; the county's challenge platform is shown in Figure 17.4. Some of these platforms allow citizens to vote on each other's ideas and to earn "points" for every online activity they perform on the platform. In some localities these virtual points can be traded in for real-life products, such as a ride with the police chief for a day in the City of Manor, Texas.[5]

The ways open innovation platforms are used differ depending on the goals and needs of the agency or municipality. Some platforms, such as the NYC Simplicity platform, are used for internal purposes only. City employees are asked to help the city be more innovative and also save costs during major budget crunches, Table 17.1 provides an overview of open innovation platforms in operation on all levels of government.

Figure 17.3
NYC Simplicity.

Source: New York City, [NYC Simplicity project page], n.d., http://www.nyc.gov/html/simplicity/html/home/home.shtml, last accessed on October 13, 2011.

Figure 17.4
Harford County's Innovation Portal.

Source: Harford County Government, "Featured Challenge," n.d., http://harfordcountymd.spigit.com/Page/Home. Used with the permission of Harford County, Maryland.

Table 17.1
Local, State, and Federal Crowdsourcing Examples.

| | | PLATFORM OPEN TO . . . | |
| | | EMPLOYEE IDEA GENERATION | CITIZEN IDEA GENERATION |
AGENCY NAME	PLATFORM NAME		
Local government			
New York City	NYC Simplicity	✓	
Mesa, AZ	iMesa	✓	✓
Maricopa County, AZ	Idea Factory for "Rewarding Ideas"		✓
City of Manor, TX	Manor Labs		✓
Harford County, MD	Harford County Innovation portal		✓
State government			
State of Washington	Transforming Washington's Budget		✓
State of Vermont	BroadbandVT.org		✓
Federal government			
Department of Veterans Affairs	VAi2—Veterans Affairs Innovation Initiative	✓	✓
NASA	NASA Idea Central	✓	
GSA	Challenge.gov		✓

LOCATION-BASED SERVICES

Another relatively new form of crowdsourcing information from citizens is the use of location-based services, which typically rely on cell phones for delivering and collecting location information. For example, Facebook allows its users to use the "Places" function to check in at a specific geographical location and to add this tag to each status update.[6] The service then displays the geolocation on a map, helping users to find nearby friends or businesses. Twitter offers a similar location-based service.[7] Every time a user tweets about a specific event, Twitter includes location information, such as a neighborhood or town, with the tweet.[8]

Government agencies have started to capitalize on citizens' willingness to share not only specific information about an event but also their physical location. During the 2011 earthquakes and hurricanes, the U.S. Geological Survey (USGS) asked citizens to use Twitter's location service to tweet to the USGS about the felt impact of each of these natural disasters. The tweets were then displayed on the USGS Community Internet Intensity Map, providing second-by-second updates of the intensity of the earthquake in specific geographical locations (Figure 17.5). Such maps can also incorporate eyewitness assessments covering a large geographical area, thereby assisting in the prioritization of emergency response and damage assessment.

Another social media service in rising use among governments is foursquare. Foursquare provides a way to brand a specific product or location for agencies that want to stay in touch with their customers or citizens. Citizens are using the geolocation function of their cell phones to check in at locations, such as polling locations, libraries, or historical sites, and to distribute that information to their friends on other social networking sites. For every *check-in* at a specific location, users earn points, badges (Figure 17.6), and so-called mayorships to reward and motivate their participation. At every check-in location, users leave comments and tips about the location and share this information with others.

The social media team at the U.S. National Archives and Records Administration (NARA) was one of the first government agencies in the United States to use foursquare in order to attract visitors to its physical and online locations.[9] NARA uses a foursquare web landing page (Figure 17.7), as well as foursquare's smartphone applications, to share tips from knowledge matter experts and citizens about documents and their physical locations around the country. Experts create tips and educational material for specific physical locations, such as historical sites in Boston, New York City, Philadelphia, and Washington, DC, and citizens can learn more about those locations with every foursquare check-in.

For example, a recent NARA initiative involving the presidential libraries and called "Walk with the Presidents on Foursquare" (Figure 17.8) guided foursquare users through the historic events and documents of past U.S. presidents. Users

Figure 17.5
USGS Asked Citizens: "Did You Feel It?"

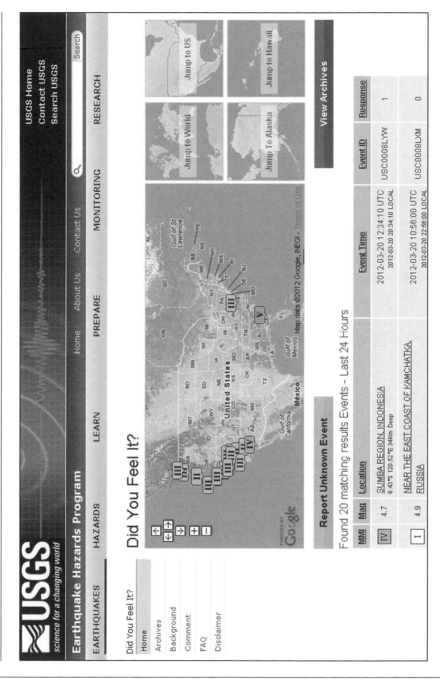

Source: U.S. Geological Survey, "USGS Community Internet Intensity Map: Virginia," August 2011, http://earthquake.usgs.gov/earthquakes/dyfi/events/se/082311a/us/index.html.

learned about historical sites, major speeches, dedications, and events, and also fun facts such as secret code names of past presidents and their favorite restaurants.

The use of foursquare fits into NARA's overall social media strategy to engage, collaborate, and build communities around records and documents. Here are NARA's core values for using social media:

OUR CORE VALUES FOR SOCIAL MEDIA

Collaboration: Together as one NARA and as partners with the public to accomplish our mission

Leadership: Out in front among government agencies and cultural institutions

Initiative: An agency of leaders who are passionate, innovative, and responsible

Diversity: Making NARA a great place to work by respecting diversity and all voices

Community: Caring about and focusing on the government community, citizen archivists, and each other

Openness: Creating an open NARA with an authentic voice[10]

Figure 17.7
NARA's Landing Page on Foursquare.

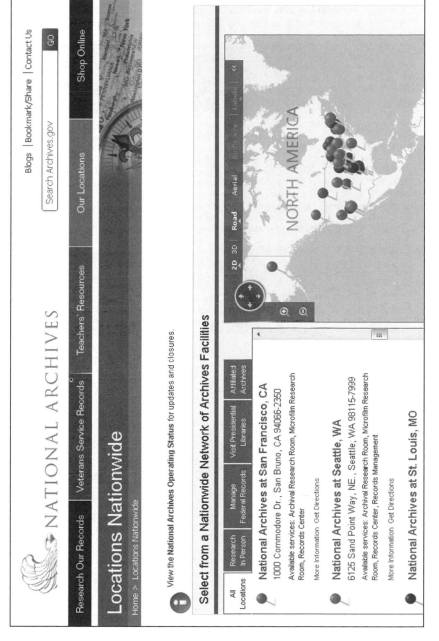

Source: U.S. National Archives and Records Administration, "The National Archives on Foursquare," n.d., http://www.archives.gov/locations/.

NARA currently uses foursquare tips only to link to existing records already
scheduled for archiving. The agency considers foursquare updates to be tempo-
rary records that are not subject to archiving.[11] NARA discusses social media
records management on its *Records Express* blog[12] and also in NARA Bulletin
2011-02.[13]

San Francisco's Bay Area Rapid Transit (BART) uses foursquare much as
NARA does, encouraging its riders to use foursquare and other location-based
services to share tips about events located near stations. A 2010 survey showed
that 38 percent of BART riders say that their use of foursquare makes riding
"more fun."[14] Riders can earn the badges shown in Figure 17.9, which were specifically designed for BART.

VIRTUAL WORLDS

Although virtual worlds have been around for several years, we chose to
place them in this section because their use has not yet been widely adopted
in the public sector. Many federal agencies did establish an early presence in
virtual worlds such as Second Life and Reaction Grid; however, interest
in corporate-sponsored virtual worlds seems to be waning in favor of more
government-centric, private virtual worlds.

One of the most valuable aspects of working in virtual worlds is that users
are not constrained by the norms and restrictions of real life in terms of phys-
ics, physical presence, time zones, and distance. Virtual worlds suspend many of
the factors that can be a major detriment to a fully collaborative environment.

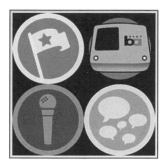
However, this feature has proven to be double-edged. Virtual worlds are typically immersive and comprehensive. In many ways the opportunities are limited solely by a user's imagination and perseverance. However, with this flexibility comes an extensive tool set that can be daunting to master. The complexity of virtual world environments also significantly limits their reach as compared to the more ubiquitous social media tools. Virtual worlds also typically require significantly more computing power than other tools do. Information-dense graphics, data feeds, and communication channels can strain older processors. Additionally, many government organizations simply block access altogether to virtual worlds because most agency firewall applications classify them as games.

Government agencies that are able to overcome or otherwise adapt to these constraints have found virtual worlds to be an excellent tool for collaboration, training, modeling, simulation, recruitment, and technology outreach. In March of 2011, the government social media group MuniGov 2.0 conducted a mock city council meeting using the virtual world of Second Life, in an effort to illustrate the ways in which local governments could enable a more effective connection between themselves and the citizens they serve via technology.

We believe that virtual worlds are a subset of social media worth watching. They are still well below critical mass in terms of popularity and ease of use, yet their potential to create truly immersive opportunities for communication and community building may very well make them more popular services in the future. As the technology advances and becomes more accessible to the general public, we may very well see virtual worlds starring in the next phase of democracy via technology.

THE MANOR STORY

Dustin Haisler
Director of Government Innovation, Spigit.com
Former Assistant City Manager and Chief Information Officer (CIO) for the City of Manor, Texas

In 2006, I began a journey with the City of Manor that would later redefine my views on innovation and government and their ability to coexist together. Manor, Texas, is a small community of roughly 8,500 people, located on the outskirts of the City of Austin. During the past six years Manor has been on the cutting edge of technology and innovation in government. Below you will find a few examples of some of the most innovative projects run by the City of Manor.

QR-Codes

One of Manor's most visible technological innovations was its QR-code program. QR-codes are two-dimensional barcodes that can be read with most newer model camera phones. Manor's QR-code program was born out of a document management project that started in 2008. The City Manager, Phil Tate, and I found QR-codes an interesting technology to bridge citizen interaction with physical objects. As a result, we deployed the first fifteen QR-coded signs throughout the city on a variety of different landmarks and projects. The project expanded into multiple new-use cases including a formal collaboration with the University of Trento, Italy, on a semantic framework for the technology. As a result of Manor's use of QR-codes, many other agencies have deployed similar programs for added transparency, asset management and tourism.

Social Media

Most people don't realize this, but Manor's first stance on social media was not a favorable one. At this point, I shared many of the corporate views that framed social media as a detractor from real work. Although I didn't take it very seriously at the time, this started to change as I became more aware of what social networks were capable of producing. I gradually realized that citizens were using social media to communicate information about our community regardless of our formal policies on social media. Meaning, whether we liked it or not, social media was a new communication tool that our citizens were using to communicate with each other and to share information regarding our community. If we did not formally engage in social media we would be the only party that was not a part of the conversation. As a result of this shift in view, Manor began to experiment with different ways to use social media to engage with the public. We tested everything from council meeting notices to emergency communications. As a result of these experiments, we had a newfound appreciation of the role social technologies would play in government for the foreseeable future.

CONCLUSION

As we have explained throughout the pages of this field guide, social media use is not about technology. It is about harnessing the value of two-way communication and finding ways to align this communication with the goals of your organization. For people working in government, social media can become a major conduit of service, guiding decisions and providing opportunities for engagement with colleagues and with citizens where they truly matter. Social media have the power to become solid collaboration tools and permanent loops of information sharing and feedback. They enable us to connect with varying constituencies, partner agencies, and other relevant resources in affordable, efficient, and productive ways.

In closing, we offer the following nine guidelines for using social media appropriately and effectively to support your organization's mission.

Approach the tools with cautious optimism. Social media are not going to be the cure-all elixir that solves all government communication and participation issues. In order to be effective with social media, you must have a solid understanding of your own organization. Be certain that you know its mission, its assets, its culture, and its audience(s). Be realistic about what the concepts and tools we've discussed in this book can do for your agency. They are very powerful and have tremendous potential if used in the right circumstances, but be sure you understand how and where they make the most sense for your organization. We suggest approaching the topic in a tool-agnostic manner: don't use social media for the sake of using the technology; instead, think about the topics and issues you want to tackle and then see where the audience you want is available to interact with your organization.

There is no one-size-fits-all social media solution for government agencies. Throughout this text we've shared ideas, concepts, and myriad examples that may spark ideas within your own organization. Take time and care in developing a social media strategy that will provide long-term success.

Be ready and willing to lose control. Social media flourish through the delegation of content development and distribution. The creation, timing, frequency, channels, format, and destination of information and specific communications are becoming much more organic than any of us have seen in the past. This can be a daunting proposition for those of us who are used to a more structured approach to communication. Focus on the larger aspects of message management. Provide the tools, the guidance, and the general expectations of your organization, and then you can slowly (but steadily) enable communication freedoms.

Do your homework. Remember that you are not alone in your efforts. You are not the first person tasked with developing a social media movement within a government agency. Many of your peers at all levels of government are heading down the same path, overcoming the same obstacles and learning the very same lessons. Use that shared experience to your advantage. Find out where others are in establishing a social media presence and what they've done. What questions did they already answer? What mistakes did they make that you can now avoid? Join a social media peer group. Voice your concerns, share your ideas … ask for help!

Match the tools to the mission. In Part Two of this guide we discussed several of the most popular tools in the public sector today, including social network services, microblogs, blogs, and wikis. Yet there are dozens of other tools and applications available today in the social media realm. Don't get caught up in the unproductive whirlwind of implementing these tools simply because you can. First, identify your organization's mission, goals, and strategy, and then consider the tools available that will best help you to enable the strategy, reach the goals, and fulfill the mission.

Create a team approach. By their most basic definition, social media are about people and groups. Successful implementation of a social media strategy within your organization requires a team effort. You'll need a team of engaged participants drawn from many parts of the organization. These people do not need to be agency leaders per se, but rather the rock stars in your organization, those who may already be engaged in social media outside of work and who need little convincing to participate in this new endeavor (see Section Sixteen). Find those people who interact directly with your organization's audience and stakeholders on a regular basis, and gather their voices at the table as you develop and deploy your social media efforts. Keep your crucial key players in the loop so there are no surprises or showstoppers as you build momentum and advocacy across your organization.

Start with some controlled experiments. Don't get too wrapped up in the development of policy and procedure before you have demonstrated qualitative or quantitative results. Take a measured approach, and identify opportunities for quick wins. By starting small you can claim some quick victories. Use these successes to advocate for larger use and acceptance of social media across the organization. Conduct experiments in a parallel time frame to the establishment of social media policy, strategy, and use across the organization. When you have built a business case, go brag about it, and secure additional resources!

Guide (but trust) your people. Social media often create a blurring of the traditional lines between work and leisure. The casual behaviors that accompany social media encourage individuals to grant accessibility to a friendly tone and a personal touch when it comes to communication. It is vital to establish guidelines for the personal use of social media. Provide guidance for the employees of your organization, rather than attempting to control their use of social media. Clearly define expectations but manage the exceptions on a case-by-case basis through your agency's disciplinary process. Taking a heavy-handed "don't do this, don't do that" approach is liable to impair creativity and success.

Don't become complacent. Social media have created an entirely new category of communication, one drastically different from traditional media opportunities. It is very difficult to predict the future of social media. The concepts and strategies described in this book will continue to shift as new ideas and examples are born. New tools will rise to the top of the heap. With every creative organization and inventive mind that evolves, social media will continue to thrive, expand, and diversify.

Likewise, your agency's approach to social media should continue to be organic. Don't let it get stale. Be sure that your strategy is flexible so that it can evolve to suit your agency's changing needs and the new tools and concepts that have yet to appear. Conduct frequent reality checks to ensure that your tools and approaches are serving the overall mission and strategy: listen to your audience and their needs. Social media use truly is about the journey. If you feel as though your efforts have reached an end, then it is probably time to redefine the strategy and set higher expectations and goals.

Keep the conversation going. Connect with your peers and network with others in your job type, your agency, or at a similar level of government. Research and review best practices and case studies to find positive examples, and identify pitfalls to avoid. Join networks like GovLoop and MuniGov. Share your personal and, when appropriate, professional content on reliable resources like LinkedIn.

If you want to know more about the latest in social media innovations in government, please follow us online at our blogs: inesmergel.wordpress.com and www.billgreeves.com. We'll continue to post new examples and the latest news on the topic of social media in the public sector. We would also love to hear your feedback on your own experiences in social media so that we can share with others and keep the dialogue going.

GLOSSARY

Accountability   The acknowledgment or assumption of responsibility for actions, decisions, or products presented.

Blogroll   A blogger's compilation of other blogs that are recommended sources. Blogrolls are usually listed in the sidebar of a blog.

Citizen engagement   The process of connecting citizens more directly with government decision making, enabling them to influence public policy and programs.

Cluster   A group of people within a social network who are connected to one another, but who have few connections with the rest of the network.

Collaboration   Working together to reach common goals through sharing knowledge and learning and building consensus.

Core   The inner group of people who do most of the work in a social network.

Crowdsourcing   Outsourcing a task to a relatively large group of people, each of whom contributes to the end result. Social media tools help to engage people in crowdsourcing activities such as collecting intelligence (as We Are Media does), co-creation (as the Humane Society of the United States's public service announcement video contest does), or voting and fundraising (as America's Giving Challenge does).

Digital natives   Members of the Millennial Generation (born between 1978 and 1993) who since birth have been exposed to the Internet and a constant stream of digital technologies.

Government 2.0   The use of Web 2.0 technologies by government agencies, both internally and externally, to increase collaboration and transparency and to potentially transform the way these agencies relate to citizens and operate.

Hubs   The larger nodes within networks, meaning the people or organizations that have many connections. Hubs are the influencers in the network, the people who know everyone and are known by everyone.

Influencers   People (or websites) who have the relative reach, influence, and social capital to mobilize others. Influence can be gauged by several metrics, including the size of an influencer's network, the number of comments on his or her blog, site traffic, and so forth.

Instant messaging (IM)   Real-time text communication between one or more people via the Internet or a mobile device. Although these conversations function like those in a chat room, IM can take place in pop-up windows on a wide range of websites or by means of an independent application (for example, Meebo).

Listening and measurement tools   Social media tools for assessing websites and online conversations. Most are available free of charge, including the following:

Real Simple Syndication (RSS)   RSS is a subscription tool used to deliver feeds (updates) from user specified blogs and other websites. FeedBurner is a popular tool used to track the number of subscribers to organizational and personal blogs.

RSS reader   An aggregation tool that collects feeds from all user-specified websites (e-mail is another delivery option). Popular RSS readers include Netvibes and Google Reader.

Search engines   Search engines index and rank websites to help Internet users find relevant content through keyword searches. Most search engines favor content that is embedded with URLs and regularly updated, tagged, and linked to from other websites. This content usually has greater search visibility (a higher position in search results).

- Traditional search engines (for example, Google and Yahoo) search all public online content (current and historical).

- Blog search engines search the last six months of blogs and blog posts. Technorati and BlogPulse are two examples of blog search engines.

(Google Blog Search allows searches for content older than six months.) A keyword search on Technorati yields related blogs and blog posts and provides the blog's rank and *authority* (the number of inbound links to that blog).

- Message board search engines search the last six months of discussion forums, threads, and posts. Examples are BoardReader and BoardTracker.
- Twitter Search allows users to search by keyword or hashtag.

Social bookmarking   A way of saving and categorizing links using tags. Whereas traditional bookmarks are saved in the web browser on a personal computer, social bookmarks are accessible from any Internet connection. Additionally, sites that help manage social bookmarks (for example, Delicious.com and StumbleUpon) allow tagged content to be searched and shared.

Tags   User-generated tags allow labeling of online content with codes or keywords. Tags can be general or specific. The more often a specific tag appears (for example, WeAreMedia) the higher it will appear in search engine results and social bookmarking sites. On Twitter, the tagging convention prefixes all tags with a hash mark (for example, #WeAreMedia). These hashtags distinguish tags from other tweeted text.

Tag cloud   A weighted, visual list of the tags in a specific website. In a tag cloud, the size of the tag is proportional to its use, with the most popular tags appearing the largest.

Website analytics   Data about a website's traffic, such as number of unique visitors and page views. Google Analytics is a robust and free analytics tool that helps users analyze and optimize websites, including blogs. PostRank measures additional engagement metrics for blogs, such as comments, bookmarks, and subscriptions.

Nodes   People or organizations connected in a social network.

Power law of distribution   Describes the imbalance between the small number of people in a network who do most of the work on a project and the remaining large number of people who do little. It is otherwise commonly known as the 80/20 rule.

Social media The peer-to-peer communication and user-generated content made possible through the advent of participatory Web 2.0 tools such as blogs, online social networks, multimedia, sites, and text messaging.

Blog Short for *web log*, a platform that allows an author (a *blogger*) to publish content online. Blog content—whether text, photos, videos, or podcasts—is organized by categories and tags. This content is viewed in reverse chronological order in successive blog posts. Others can leave comments on these posts. Millions of blogs exist, and this set of social media is often referred to as the *blogosphere*.

Listserv An electronic mailing list that distributes messages to subscribers via e-mail. Listservs are usually topical, and in most cases allow anyone to reply or to send a message to the group.

Microblog A blog composed of "brief text updates or micromedia such as photos or audio clips. . . . These messages can be submitted by a variety of means, including text messaging, instant messaging, e-mail, digital audio, or the web" (see http://en.wikipedia.org/wiki/Micro_blog). Twitter is a popular microblogging platform that limits text-based tweets (posts) to 140 characters.

Multimedia Nontext-based digital content, from MP3s to videos to photos, that can be published, shared, and tagged online. Online music-sharing sites include Napster and iTunes. Online video-sharing sites include YouTube, Vimeo, and Google Video. Online photo-sharing sites include Flickr, Picasa, and Photobucket.

Social networks Online communities of individuals (nodes) who are connected to each other via ties (friending, following, group membership, and so on). Social networks form through many types of social media platforms, including blog networks, listservs, and Google Groups. Larger social networks, such as Facebook, MySpace, and LinkedIn, serve a wide variety of interests and geographical areas. Niche social networks, such as Change.org and independent Ning networks, are typically focused on a specific topic.

Social news site A website, such as Digg, that enables people to submit and rank news stories, listing the most popular stories first.

Virtual world   A computer-simulated environment—or cyber world—that enables users to interact with each other and manipulate the digital ecosystem via their personalized avatars (Second Life is a well-known virtual world).

Wiki   A website that can be easily edited by many people simultaneously, allowing them to think, strategize, share documents, and create plans together. Wikis facilitate microplanning, the process of enabling more people to participate in the creation and implementation of an effort much less expensively over longer periods of time than would otherwise be possible.

Social media policy   Organizational guidelines for participating in social media. Policies often include hard-and-fast rules for confidentiality, disclaimers, and disclosures in order to protect the organization, employees, and stakeholders, but should ultimately facilitate effective and authentic social media engagement. Blogging guidelines might include best practices. A comment policy might include criteria for blog comments (for example, no profanity).

Social media strategy   An organizational approach to using social media to increase collaboration and innovation.

Ties   The connections between people and organizations, or nodes, in a social network.

Transparency   Honest and authentic information, communication, and actions. Transparency is a core tenet of social media engagement, requiring disclosure of affiliations and biases that—if omitted—could diminish credibility. Organizations that have transparency as a fundamental value are called *transparents*.

Uniform resource locator (URL)   A web address. Also referred to as *links*, URLs are often embedded in hyperlinked text on websites to enable click-throughs to other websites.

Viral   A term used to describe the organic and rapid spread of online content resulting from many individuals engaging in electronic communication.

Web 1.0   The first era of the Internet, which began in the early 1990s with the advent of the World Wide Web and e-mail.

Web 2.0   The second era of the Internet, starting in the late 1990s, through which online information became inexpensively storable, shareable, and participatory through the advent of social media tools.

ADDITIONAL RESOURCES

Boyd, D. M., & Ellison, N. B. (2007). Social network sites: definition, history, and scholarship. *Journal of Computer-Mediated Communication*, *13*(1). Retrieved from http://jcmc.indiana.edu/vol13/issue1/boyd.ellison.html

Bretschneider, S. I., & Mergel, I. (2010). Technology and public management information systems: Where we have been and where we are. In D. C. Menzel & H. J. White (Eds.), *The state of public administration: Issues, challenges, and opportunities* (pp. 187–203). New York: M. E. Sharpe.

Christensen, C. M., & Overdorf, M. (2000, March–April). Meeting the challenge of disruptive change. *Harvard Business Review*, pp. 65–76.

Corrin, A. (2011, January 14). DOD social media rules to expire soon: Deployed troops using Facebook and Twitter might suffer loss of access. *DefenseSystems*. Retrieved from http://defensesystems.com/articles/2011/01/14/dod-social-media-policy-in-limbo.aspx

Crovitz, G. (2011, February 14). Egypt's revolution by social media. *Wall Street Journal*. Retrieved from http://online.wsj.com/article/SB10001424052748703 786804576137980252177072.html

Franks, P. C. (2010). *How federal agencies can effectively manage records created using new social media tools*. Washington, DC: IBM Center for The Business of Government. Retrieved from http://www.businessofgovernment .org/report/how-federal-agencies-can-effectively-manage-records-created-using-new-social-media-tools

Kettl, D. (2006). Managing boundaries in American administration: The collaboration imperative. *Public Administration Review*, *66*(Suppl. 1), 10–19.

Library of Congress. (2010, April 15). Twitter donates entire tweet archive to Library of Congress. Retrieved from http://www.loc.gov/today/pr/2010/10-081.html

McGirt, E. (2009, April 1). How Chris Hughes helped launch Facebook and the Barack Obama campaign. *FastCompany*. Retrieved from http://www.fastcompany.com/magazine/134/boy-wonder.html

Mergel, I. (2010). Government 2.0 revisited: Social media strategies in the public sector. *PA Times*, *33*(3), 7, 10. Retrieved from http://faculty.maxwell.syr.edu/iamergel/files/Gov20_Revisited_2010.pdf

Mississippi Department of Information Technology Services. (2010, December 31). *State of Mississippi: Strategic master plan for information technology 2011–2013*. Retrieved from http://www.its.ms.gov/docs/MS%20MasterPlan.pdf

National Association of State Chief Information Officers. (2011, January 5). NASCIO and attorneys general negotiate model Facebook agreement for state government use. Retrieved from http://www.nascio.org/newsroom/pressrelease.cfm?id=93

Obama, B. (2009). Transparency and open government (Memorandum for the heads of executive departments and agencies). Retrieved from http://www.whitehouse.gov/the_press_office/TransparencyandOpenGovernment

Office of Management and Budget. (2010, April 7). Social media, web-based interactive technologies, and the Paperwork Reduction Act (Memorandum for the heads of executive departments and agencies and independent regulatory agencies). Retrieved from http://www.whitehouse.gov/sites/default/filcs/omb/assets/inforeg/SocialMediaGuidance_04072010.pdf

Office of Management and Budget. (2010, June 25). Guidance for agency use of third-party websites and applications (Memorandum for the heads of executive departments and agencies). Retrieved from http://www.whitehouse.gov/sites/default/filcs/omb/assets/memoranda_2010/m10-23.pdf

O'Reilly, T. (2005, September 30). *What is Web 2.0: Design patterns and business models for the next generation of software*. Retrieved from http://www.oreillynet.com/pub/a/oreilly/tim/news/2005/09/30/what-is-web-20.html

Palfrey, J., & Gasser, U. (2008). *Born digital: Understanding the first generation of digital natives*. New York: Basic Books.

Pew Research Center for the People & the Press. (2010, April 18). *Distrust, discontent, anger and partisan rancor: The people and their government*. Retrieved from http://pewresearch.org/pubs/1569/trust-in-government-distrust-discontent-anger-partisan-rancor

Rainie, L., & Purcell, K. (2010, March 15). *The economics of online news*. Pew Internet & American Life Project. Retrieved from http://www.pewinternet .org/Reports/2010/5—The-economics-of-online-news.aspx

Rainie, L., & Purcell, K. (2011, March 1). *How the public perceives community information services*. Pew Internet & American Life Project. Retrieved from http://www.pewinternet.org/Reports/2011/08-Community-Information-Systems/1-Report/10-Citizen-info-search-strategies.aspx

Sen, A. K. (2011, February 27). Gadhafi hits social media, Blames youths for spreading revolution. *Washington Times*. Retrieved from http://www .washingtontimes.com/news/2011/feb/27/gadhafi-hits-social-media

Singer, P. (2011, February 1). *What does the next generation of American leaders think?* Washington, DC: Brookings Institution. Retrieved from http://www .brookings.edu/reports/2011/02_young_leaders_singer.aspx

Smith, A. (2010, August 11). *Home broadband 2010*. Pew Internet & American Life Project. Retrieved from http://www.pewinternet.org/Reports/2010/Home-Broadband-2010.aspx

State of Nebraska, Nebraska Information Technology Commission, Standards and Guidelines. (2011, July 12). *Social media guidelines* (NITC 4-205). Retrieved from http://www.nitc.ne.gov/standards/4-205.html

Stelter, B. (2008, July 7). The Facebooker who friended Obama. *New York Times*. Retrieved from http://www.nytimcs.com/2008/07/07/technology/07hughes.html

Surowiecki, J. (2004). *The wisdom of crowds: Why the many are smarter than the few and how collective wisdom shapes business, economies, societies and nations*. New York: Doubleday.

Teitell, B. (2011, March 27). Connected, exhausted: Texting teenagers who stay "on call" all night pay the price in lost sleep. *Boston Globe*. Retrieved from http://www.boston.com/community/moms/articles/2011/03/27/on_call_all_ night_can_leave_texting_teens_tired_out

U.S. Department of the Interior. (2011, May 2). *The DOI social media guidebook*. Retrieved from http://www.doi.gov/notices/upload/DOI-Social-Media-Guidebook-2011-05-02.pdf

U.S. General Services Administration. (2010, March 25). *Landmark agreements clear path for government new media* (GSA #10572). Retrieved from http:// www.gsa.gov/portal/content/103496

U.S. General Services Administration. (2011, June 22). Terms of service agreements: GSA paves the way for government use of new media. Retrieved from http://www.gsa.gov/portal/content/104320

U.S. National Archives and Records Administration. (2010, October 20). Guidance on managing records in Web 2.0/social media platforms (NARA Bulletin 2012-02). Retrieved from http://www.archives.gov/records-mgmt/bulletins/2011/2011-02.html

Utah Department of Technology Services. (2009, October 12). *State of Utah social media guidelines*. Retrieved from http://www.utahta.wikispaces.net/file/view/State+of+Utah+Social+Media+Guidelines+9.29.pdf

Wesch, M. (2007, March 8). *The machine is us/ing us* [YouTube video]. Retrieved from http://www.youtube.com/watch?v=NLlGopyXT_g

N O T E S

PART ONE

1. J. N. Hoover, "FEMA to Use Social Media for Emergency Response," *InformationWeek*, January 19, 2011, http://www.informationweek.com/ news/government/info-management/showArticle.jhtml?articleID= 229000918.

SECTION ONE

1. National Center for Missing & Exploited Children, [Department of Justice press conference], Facebook DC live, 2011, http://www.livestream .com/facebookdclive/video?clipId=pla_5d19d270-9f84-4a2b-b7f9- 4539e9ccb122&utm_source=lslibrary&utm_medium=ui-thumb.

2. M. McHugh, "Facebook Will Start Sending Amber Alerts to Users: Users Will Now Be Able to View State-Specific Amber Alert Notifications," *Digital Trends*, April 4, 2011, http://www.digitaltrends.com/social-media/ facebook-will-start-sending-amber-alerts-to-users.

3. Associated Press, "Report: Internet Has Transformed the News Industry," May 14, 2011, http://www.pewinternet.org/Media-Mentions/2011/Internet- usage-transforming-news-industry.aspx.

4. See, for example, T. O'Reilly, *What Is Web 2.0? Design Patterns and Business Models for the Next Generation of Software*, September 30, 2005, http://www.oreillynet.com/pub/a/oreilly/tim/news/2005/09/30/what-is- web-20.html.

5. A. Watters, "The Web (Finally) Surpasses Newspapers as Source for Americans' News," ReadWriteWeb, 2011, http://www.readwriteweb.com/archives/milestone_the_web_finally_surpasses_newspapers_as.php.

6. B. Greeves, "Social Media & Emergency Management," *Greever's Den*, March 21, 2011, http://billgreeves.com/2011/03/21/mapping-the-social-media-response-in-japan.

7. See, for example, A. K. Sen, "Gadhafi Hits Social Media, Blames Youths for Spreading Revolution," *Washington Times*, February 27, 2011, and L. G. Crovitz, "Egypt's Revolution by Social Media," *Wall Street Journal*, February 14, 2011.

8. See J. Chang, "U.S. Army Social and Mobile—Victories and Challenges," Blog Talk Radio, March 13, 2011, http://www.blogtalkradio.com/gov20/2011/03/14/us-army-social-and-mobile-victories-and-challenges.

SECTION TWO

1. See N. Augenstein, "Amtrak Power and Communication Lines Falter," WTOP, August 24, 2010, http://www.wtop.com/?nid=25&sid=2034708.

2. M. Wesch, "The Machine Is Us/ing Us" [YouTube video], 2007, http://www.youtube.com/watch?v=NLlGopyXT_g.

3. For more information on USGS Citizen Scientists, see U.S. Geological Survey, "Congressional Briefing—Citizen Science and Earthquakes: Reducing the Risk Through the Power of People," May 12, 2010, http://www.usgs.gov/newsroom/article.asp?ID=2460.

SECTION THREE

1. D. Kettl, "Managing Boundaries in American Administration: The Collaboration Imperative," *Public Administration Review* 66, suppl. 1 (2006): 10–19.

2. Pew Research Center for the People & the Press, *Distrust, Discontent, Anger and Partisan Rancor: The People and Their Government*, April 18, 2010, http://pewresearch.org/pubs/1569/trust-in-government-distrust-discontent-anger-partisan-rancor.

3. L. Rainie and K. Purcell, *The Economics of Online News*, Pew Internet & American Life Project, 2010, http://www.pewinternet.org/Reports/2010/5-The-economics-of-online-news.aspx.

4. L. Rainie and K. Purcell, *How the Public Perceives Community Information Services*, Pew Internet & American Life Project, 2011, http://www.pewinternet.org/Reports/2011/08-Community-Information-Systems/1-Report/10-Citizen-info-search-strategies.aspx.

SECTION FOUR

1. For more information, see E. Perlman, "Working in Wiki: How to Assemble Real Ideas in a Virtual World," Governing, April 30, 2008, http://www.governing.com/topics/technology/Working-in-Wiki.html, and C. G. Lynch, "How Vivek Kundra Fought Government Waste One Google App at a Time," *CIO*, September 22, 2008, http://www.cio.com/article/450636/How_Vivek_Kundra_Fought_Government_Waste_One_Google_App_At_a_Time.

2. S. I. Bretschneider and I. Mergel, "Technology and Public Management Information Systems: Where We Have Been and Where We Are Going," in *The State of Public Administration: Issues, Challenges, and Opportunities*, ed. D. C. Menzel and H. J. White (New York: M. E. Sharpe, 2010), 187–203.

3. D. M. Boyd and N. B. Ellison, "Social Network Sites: Definition, History, and Scholarship," *Journal of Computer-Mediated Communication* 13, no. 1 (2007), http://jcmc.indiana.edu/vol13/issue1/boyd.ellison.html.

4. U.S. General Services Administration, "Landmark Agreements Clear Path for Government New Media" (News release, GSA #10572), 2010, http://www.gsa.gov/portal/content/103496.

5. U.S. National Archives and Records Administration, *Guidance on Managing Records in Web 2.0/Social Media Platforms* (NARA Bulletin 2011-02), 2010, http://www.archives.gov/records-mgmt/bulletins/2011/2011-02.html.

6. Library of Congress, "Twitter Donates Entire Tweet Archive to Library of Congress" (News release), April 15, 2010, http://www.loc.gov/today/pr/2010/10-081.html.

7. Office of Management and Budget, "Guidance for Agency Use of Third-Party Websites and Applications" (Memorandum for the heads of executive

departments and agencies), 2010, http://www.whitehouse.gov/sites/default/files/omb/assets/memoranda_2010/m10-23.pdf, and National Association of State Chief Information Officers, "NASCIO and Attorneys General Negotiate Model Facebook Agreement for State Government Use" (Press release), 2011, http://www.nascio.org/newsroom/pressrelease.cfm?id=93.

8. C. M. Christensen and M. Overdorf, "Meeting the Challenge of Disruptive Change," *Harvard Business Review*, March/April 2000, 65–76.

SECTION FIVE

1. Apps for Democracy, "About APPS09," n.d., http://www.appsfordemocracy.org/about.

SECTION SIX

1. Cisco, *Cisco Visual Networking Index: Global Mobile Data Traffic Forecast Update, 2010–2015*, 2011, http://www.cisco.com/en/US/solutions/collateral/ns341/ns525/ns537/ns705/ns827/white_paper_c11-520862.pdf.

2. A. Smith, *Home Broadband 2010*, Pew Internet & American Life Project, 2010, http://www.pewinternet.org/Reports/2010/Home-Broadband-2010.aspx.

3. H. Weber, "With 140 Million Active Users & 340 Million Tweets per Day, Twitter Is Officially Mainstream," The Next Web, March 21, 2012, http://thenextweb.com/socialmedia/2012/03/21/twitter-has-over-140-million-active-users-sending-over-340-million-tweets-a-day.

4. B. Teitell, "Connected, Exhausted: Texting Teenagers Who Stay "On Call" All Night Pay the Price in Lost Sleep," *Boston Globe*, March 27, 2011, http://www.boston.com/community/moms/articles/2011/03/27/on_call_all_night_can_leave_texting_teens_tired_out.

5. J. Palfrey and U. Gasser, *Born Digital: Understanding the First Generation of Digital Natives* (New York: Basic Books, 2008).

6. P. Singer, *What Does the Next Generation of American Leaders Think?* Brookings Institution, 2011, http://www.brookings.edu/reports/2011/02_young_leaders_singer.aspx.

7. J. Preston, "Internet Users Turned to Social Networks in Elections, Survey Finds," *Media Decoder*, March 17, 2011, http://mediadecoder.blogs .nytimes.com/2011/03/17/internet-users-turned-to-social-networks-in-elections-survey-finds/?ref=technology.

8. E. Montalbano, "NYC to Hire Social Media Expert," *InformationWeek*, June 4, 2010, http://www.informationweek.com/news/government/state-local/showArticle.jhtml?articleID=225400061.

PART TWO

1. D. Fletcher, [Quotation], 2010, http://www.mirnabard.com/2010/04/99-favorite-social-media-quotes-and-tips.

SECTION SEVEN

1. See Facebook at https://www.facebook.com/press/info.php?statistics for up-to-date statistics.

2. See GigaOM at http://gigaom.com/2011/03/25/facebook-search-googl for a discussion of Facebook's and Google's comparative roles in assisting people to search for social information.

3. For more statistics about social media demographics, see the following websites: Inside Facebook, http://www.insidefacebook.com/2009/02/02/fastest-growing-demographic-on-facebook-women-over-55 and http://www.insidefacebook.com/2009/03/25/number-of-us-facebook-users-over-35-nearly-doubles-in-last-60-days; Inc., http://www.inc.com/news/articles/2010/08/users-over-50-are-fastest-growing-social-media-demographic.html; and Pew Internet, http://www.pewinternet.org/Reports/2010/Older-Adults-and-Social-Media.aspx.

SECTION NINE

1. H. Weber, "With 140 Million Active Users & 340 Million Tweets per Day, Twitter Is Officially Mainstream," The Next Web, March 21, 2012, http://thenextweb.com/socialmedia/2012/03/21/twitter-has-over-140-million-active-users-sending-over-340-million-tweets-a-day.

2. The quotation from Lee Rainie is used with permission.

3. For a complete overview of Web 2.0 tools used by the LAFD see H. Havenstein, "LA Fire Department All 'aTwitter' over Web 2.0," *Computerworld*, August 3, 2007, http://www.pcworld.com/article/135518/la_fire_department_all_atwitter_over_web_20.html.

4. Gov 2.0 Radio, "U.S. Army Social and Mobile," March 13, 2011, http://gov20radio.com/2011/03/us-army-social-mobile.

5. See http://www.epa.gov/epahome/socialmedia.html#Twitter for a full list of the EPA's Twitter accounts.

6. See Go.USA.gov, [URL shortener], n.d., https://go.usa.gov (login required).

SECTION TEN

1. D. Terdiman, *Study: Wikipedia as Accurate as Britannica*, CNET, 2005, http://news.cnet.com/Study-Wikipedia-as-accurate-as-Britannica/2100-1038_3-5997332.html.

2. For an up-to-date list of wiki software and a comparison of existing wiki software choices, see the following Wikipedia articles: http://en.wikipedia.org/wiki/List_of_wiki_software, and http://en.wikipedia.org/wiki/Comparison_of_wiki_software.

3. N. Cohen, "Care to Write Army Doctrine? With ID, Log On," *New York Times*, August 14, 2009, http://www.nytimes.com/2009/08/14/business/14army.html; and J. J. Carafano, "Mastering the Art of Wiki: Understanding Social Networking and National Security," *JFQ* 60 (2011, first quarter): 73–78, http://www.ndu.edu/press/social-networking-national-security.html.

4. Cohen, "Care to Write Army Doctrine?"

5. For more information on the ExpertNet wiki plan at the time it was initiated in 2010, visit the White House Blog at http://www.whitehouse.gov/blog/2010/12/29/expertnet-wiki-update.

6. According to the Wikiplanning website, http://www.wikiplanning.org/index.php?P=virtualcharrette, a *virtual charrette* is a "collaborative session in which a group of designers drafts a solution to a design problem. Charrettes often take place in multiple sessions in which the group divides

into sub-groups. Each sub-group then presents its work to the full group as material for future dialogue. Such charrettes serve as a way of generating a design solution while integrating the aptitudes and interests of a diverse group of people."

PART THREE

1. U.S. Government Accountability Office, *Social Media: Federal Agencies Need Policies and Procedures for Managing and Protecting Information They Access and Disseminate* (GAO-11-605), June 2011, http://www.gao.gov/assets/330/320244.pdf.

SECTION TWELVE

1. For more information see A. Perlut, "A Lesson from the Downfall of Anthony Weiner," *Forbes*, June, 30, 2011, http://blogs.forbes.com/marketshare/2011/06/30/a-lesson-from-the-downfall-of-anthony-weiner.

2. See http://www.epa.gov/aboutepa/whatwedo.html to learn more about the activities the EPA derives from its mission statement.

3. For a full description of the City of Hampton's social media policy, see http://itdirectors.wi.gov/docview.asp?docid=18476&locid=139.

SECTION THIRTEEN

1. For a more detailed discussion of the difference between pull and push strategies, see I. Mergel, "Government 2.0 Revisited: Social Media Strategies in the Public Sector," *PA Times* 33, no. 3 (2010):7, 10, http://faculty.maxwell.syr.edu/iamergel/files/Gov20_Revisited_2010.pdf.

2. See J. Surowiecki, *The Wisdom of Crowds: Why the Many Are Smarter Than the Few and How Collective Wisdom Shapes Business, Economies, Societies and Nations* (New York: Doubleday, 2004).

3. City and County of San Francisco, Office of the Mayor, "Mayor Lee Announces First of Its Kind Facebook Application for City Services," February 28, 2011, http://www.sfmayor.org/index.aspx?page=268.

SECTION FOURTEEN

1. GovLoop, *Web 2.0 Governance Policies and Best Practices*, n.d., http://data .govloop.com/dataset/Web-2-0-Governance-Policies-And-Best-Practices-Ref/b47r-pgph.

2. See, for example, the *Social Media Guidebook* of the Department of the Interior, May 2, 2011, http://www.doi.gov/notices/upload/DOI-Social-Media-Guidebook-2011-05-02.pdf.

3. U.S. Navy, Navy Office of Information, *Navy Command Social Media Handbook*, Fall 2010, http://www.cnrc.navy.mil/PAO/socialnetwrk/soc_med_hnd_bk.pdf.

4. See A. Corrin, "DOD Social Media Rules to Expire Soon: Deployed Troops Using Facebook and Twitter Might Suffer Loss of Access," *DefenseSystems*, January 14, 2011, http://defensesystems.com/articles/2011/01/14/dod-social-media-policy-in-limbo.aspx.

5. For an overview of how to use the TOS for your agency, see "Terms of Service Agreements: GSA Paves the Way for Government Use of New Media," at http://www.gsa.gov/portal/content/104320.

6. Read the full annual strategic plan of the State of Mississippi's Department of Information Technology Services at http://www.its.ms.gov/docs/MS%20 MasterPlan.pdf.

7. See http://www.section508.gov for more information about the requirements of the Rehabilitation Act.

8. Access the *Federal Plain Language Guidelines*, released May 2011, or download the PDF at http://www.plainlanguage.gov/howto/guidelines/FederalPLGuidelines/FederalPLGuidelines.pdf.

9. *Federal Plain Language Guidelines*, "Introduction," http://www.plainlanguage .gov/howto/guidelines/FederalPLGuidelines.

10. *Federal Plain Language Guidelines*, p. 98.

11. For an overview of the current practices see P. C. Franks, *How Federal Agencies Can Effectively Manage Records Created Using New Social Media Tools* (Washington, DC: IBM Center for The Business of Government, 2010), http://www.businessofgovernment.org/report/how-federal-agencies-can-effectively-manage-records-created-using-new-social-media-tools.

12. National Archives and Records Administration, "Guidance on Managing Records in Web 2.0/Social Media Platforms" (NARA Bulletin 2011-02), October 20, 2010, http://www.archives.gov/records-mgmt/bulletins/2011/2011-02.html.

13. City of Reno, Nevada, *Social Media Communications*, 2011, http://reno.gov/index.aspx?page=2142.

14. Utah Department of Technology Services, *State of Utah Social Media Guidelines*, 2009, http://www.utahta.wikispaces.net/file/view/State+of+Utah+Social+Media+Guidelines+9.29.pdf.

15. J. Terreri, "For Elected Officials Social Media Tools Present New Challenges," *Democrat and Chronicle*, July 16, 2011, http://rocdocs.democratandchronicle.com/delegates/article/70659.

16. State of Nebraska, Nebraska Information Technology Commission, Standards and Guidelines, *Social Media Guidelines* (NITC 4-205), 2010, http://www.nitc.ne.gov/standards/4-205.html.

SECTION FIFTEEN

1. See the discussion of plain language use in government in Section Fourteen and online at http://www.plainlanguage.gov.

2. U.S. Navy, *LinkedIn, U.S. Navy Social Media Snapshot* [Slide show], 2011, http://www.slideshare.net/USNavySocialMedia/linkedin-for-navy-personnel.

3. State of Michigan, Department of Technology, Management & Budget, *Social Media Standard*, November 30, 2011, http://www.michigan.gov/documents/som/1340.00.10_Social_Media_Standard_370668_7.pdf.

4. Reprinted with the permission of Roanoke County, Virginia.

PART FOUR

1. "Nick Schaper: Incoming Executive Director, Digital Strategic Communications at the U.S. Chamber of Commerce; Outgoing Director of Digital Media, Speaker John Boehner (R-Ohio)," *Washington Post*, 2011, http://www.washingtonpost.com/politics/nick-schaper/gIQAi41QKP_topic.html.

SECTION SEVENTEEN

1. See the full report in M. Madden and K. Zickuhr, *65% of American Adults Use Social Networking Sites*, Pew Internet & American Life Project, 2011, http://pewinternet.org/~/media//Files/Reports/2011/PIP-SNS-Update-2011.pdf.

2. I. Mergel, "The Use of Social Media to Dissolve Knowledge Silos in Government," in *The Future of Public Administration, Public Management, and Public Service Around the World: The Minnowbrook Perspective*, ed. R. O'Leary, S. Kim, and D. M. Van Slyke (Washington, DC: Georgetown University Press, 2010), 177–187, http://faculty.maxwell.syr.edu/iamergel/files/Mergel%20-%202010%20-%20Minnowbrook.pdf.

3. See for example the city planning wiki approaches discussed in I. Mergel, *Using Wikis in Government: A Guide for Public Managers* (Washington, DC: IBM Center for The Business of Government, 2011), http://www.businessofgovernment.org/report/using-wikis-government-guide-public-managers.

4. Challenge.gov, "About Challenge.gov," n.d., http://challenge.gov/about.

5. For more details on Manor, Texas, and InnoBucks, see A. Kamenetz, "How an Army of Techies Is Taking on City Hall," *FastCompany*, November 29, 2010, http://www.fastcompany.com/magazine/151/icitizen-bonus.html?page=0%2C2.

6. See http://www.facebook.com/places for an overview of how Facebook displays these data.

7. For a description of this service, see "Location, Location, Location," *Twitter Blog*, August 20, 2009, http://blog.twitter.com/2009/08/location-location-location.html.

8. For more information on how to add locations to tweets, see "What's Happening—and Where?" *Twitter Blog*, March 11, 2010, http://blog.twitter.com/2010/03/whats-happeningand-where.html.

9. National Archives and Records Administration, "The National Archives Plays Foursquare!" (Press release), February 2, 2011, http://www.archives.gov/press/press-releases/2011/nr11-64.html.

10. U.S. National Archives and Records Administration, *Social Media Strategy*, December 8, 2010, http://www.archives.gov/social-media/strategies/social-media-strategy-2010-12-08.pdf.

11. For more details about how NARA deals with foursquare records, watch the webinar "Connecting with Citizens" at http://www.usa.gov/webcontent/wmu/summer2011/connecting-citizens.shtml.

12. NARA's *Records Express* blog provides frequent updates and ongoing conversation about social media records management at http://blogs.archives.gov/records-express/?tag=web-20.

13. U.S. National Archives and Records Administration, "Guidance on Managing Records in Web 2.0/Social Media Platforms" (NARA Bulletin 2011-02), October 20, 2010, http://www.archives.gov/records-mgmt/bulletins/2011/2011-02.html.

14. Bay Area Rapid Transit, "BART/Foursquare Survey: 38% Say Foursquare Makes Riding BART 'More Fun,'" May 5, 2010, http://www.bart.gov/news/articlcs/2010/news20100505.aspx.

INDEX

Page references followed by *fig* indicates an illustrated figure; followed by *t* indicates a table.

networking presence by, 19; step-by-step guide for Twitter administration by, 63–69; tweets sent by, 59; two-way collaborative communication developed by, 20–22*fig*

Government & Social Media Wiki, 84, 87*fig*

Government websites: blogs integrated with, 9, 11*t*, 49, 51; content development of first generation of, 8, 9*fig*; e-mail comments left on, 7–8; future social media applications to, 149–163; HowTo.gov, 84, 86*fig*; social media sites integrated into, 9, 11*t*

GovLoop.com: creation of, 17; description and functions of, 43, 44*fig*; as networking tactic, 104; overview of government use of, 39*t*; Steve Ressler on the story of, 43, 45–46

Greenversations blog (EPA), 56

Greeves, Bill, 9

H

Haisler, Dustin, 162–163

Hampton (Virginia), 99

Harford County's innovation portal, 152, 154*fig*

#hashtags. *See* Twitter #hashtags

Health Data Palooza, 25

HowTo.gov website, 84, 86*fig*

H/T or HT (head tip or heard through) tweets, 63

Human resources and workforce development, 143

Hyperlinks, 71

I

Information: Freedom of Information Act (FOIA) governing, 119; how social media has changed communication of, 8–9; microblogging to distribute mission-relevant, 59–69; RT (retweeting) of, 63; social media channels as adding new outlets for, 9, 10, 11*fig*; social media policies on keeping records and collecting, 119–121; social media tactic for education and sharing, 103, 104*fig*; wikis used to share, 74–81*fig*

Information technology workgroup, 142

Internet: Google search engine for the, 32, 38, 39*t*; as primary daily news resource, 4; social search engines for the, 38, 67–68

Internet & American Life Project (Pew Research Center), 60

J

Japanese earthquake (2011), 4

K

Kundra, Vivek, 17

L

Law enforcement: Amber Alert Facebook page, 3; Boynton Beach (FL) Police Department case study on, 84, 88–92

Lee, Ed, 106

Legal counsel workgroup, 142

Library of Congress Twitter Archive, 18, 19

Limited public forums, 124

LinkedIn: communication functions of, 37; communities of, 4; description and functions of, 43; government website integrated with, 9, 11*fig*; overview of government use of, 39*t*; U.S. Navy policy on personal use of, 131

Live town hall meetings: community building through, 104, 105*fig*;

of, 4; developing strategies for using, 95–101; expansion into everyday life, 4–5; implementation of strategy and tactics for using, 141–146; integration into government websites, 9, 11*t*; personal versus professional use of, 129–139; public sector future of, 149–163; recognizing (and minimizing) costs of using, 144–145; recommendations for getting the most out of, 165–168; role of in Arab Spring (2011), 5; tactics for using, 103–108*fig*. *See also* Content; Government 2.0; Technology

Social media ambassadors, 144

Social media drivers: connectedness as, 31–32; cost reductions through social media tools as, 33; expectations of digital natives as, 32–33; summary of, 34

Social Media Guidelines (Nebraska), 113, 114*fig*

Social media policies: for branding to establish "corporate" identity, 112–113, 114*fig*; defining organizational responsibility through, 110, 112; ensuring accessibility of social media content, 117–118; focusing on providing clear guidance, 109–110; for legitimate business purposes only, 109; growing need for social media strategy and, 95–96; on keeping records and collecting public information, 119–121*fig*; listing of all acceptable platforms as part of, 113; *Navy Command Social Media Handbook,* 110, 111*fig*; Nebraska's *Social Media Guidelines* example of, 113, 114*fig*; on posting a blog, 52–53; on setting a content and information

approval process, 116–117; on setting acceptable personal use, 131–134; on setting commenting policy and ensuring online netiquette, 121–126; on using plain language online, 118; on using social media for two-way communications, 116; summary review on recommendations for, 126–127; *The Ventura City Manager Blog* comment policy, 52–53, 54*fig*

Social media strategy: building your organization's audiences with, 100–101; focusing on mission support, 96–98; growing need for policies and, 95–96; identifying your organization's audiences using, 98–100; implementation of, 141–146; rolling documents on, 95; summary review of recommendations for, 101

Social media tactics: citizen participation and engagement through community building, 103–104, 105*fig*; implementation of, 141–146; information and education, 103, 104*fig*; networking, 104, 106, 107*fig*; transactional, 106, 108*fig*

Social media tools: approaching with cautious optimism, 165–166; begin with controlled experiments on using, 167; and being willing to lose control of content, 166; Boynton Beach (FL) Police Department use of, 88–92; choosing the right, 83–92; cost reductions through sophisticated, 33; creating a team approach to using, 166–167; do your homework on, 166; guiding your people in the use of, 167; keeping the conversation going on using, 168; matrix for matching government needs to, 84, 85*t*, 166;

Japanese earthquake and tsunami (2011) responses on, 4; Kristy Fifelski's personal account disclaimer on, 135*fig*; Library of Congress Twitter Archive, 18, 19*fig*; location-based service of, 156; Los Angeles Fire Department (LAFD) updates and alerts on, 60, 61*fig*; Macon Phillips's account on, 120, 121*fig*; used as parallel publishing stream, 59; social media policy for two-way communications on, 116; social search engine function of, 67–68; step-by-step guide for administration of, 63–69; @TheirAccountName, 64; USGS tracking of citizen tweets during earthquakes, 9; White House Twitter account, 69. *See also* Microblogging

Twitter #hashtags: description of Twitter, 64–65; EPA tweet including @mentions and, 66*fig*; #FF (#Follow Friday) update, 65, 67*fig*; #gov20 and #opengov, 64; trending topics created from popular, 65

Twitter love, 65

U

URL shorteners, 67

U.S. Army's Tactics, Techniques, and Procedures (TTP) wiki, 76

U.S. Department of Health and Human Services (HHS), 25

U.S. Environmental Protection Agency (EPA): Apps for the Environment, 25; *Greenversations* blog of the, 56, 57*fig*; mission statement of the, 96–97*fig*, 98; social media tactics for sharing information and education, 103, 104*fig*; social media used to identify audiences of the, 98–100; strategic communication and interaction objectives of the, 99*t*; tweet including @mentions and #hashtag, 66*fig*; Twitter accounts hosted by, 67; Twitter list for EPA region 9, 68*fig*; Twitter update by, 104*fig*

U.S. Federal Communications Commission (FCC Connect's social media branding), 115*fig*

U.S. General Services Administration (GSA): BetterBuy project wiki of the, 79, 81*fig*, 104, 107*fig*; Challenge. gov created by, 150, 151*fig*, 152*fig*; Federal Web Managers Council of, 84; GovLoop.com used to discuss Acquisition 2.0 effort by, 104, 107*fig*; HowTo.gov website by, 84, 86*fig*; Office of Citizen Services and Innovative Technologies of, 84; RFPs (requests for proposals) crowdsourced by, 104, 106; terms of service agreements (TOS) negotiated by, 18, 113

U.S. Geological Survey (USGS): comment policy of the, 122, 123*fig*; Community Internet Intensity Map "Did You Feel It?," 156, 157*fig*; location-based service by, 156; tracking citizen tweets during earthquakes, 9

U.S. Justice Department, 3

U.S. National Archives and Records Administration (NARA): core values for social media of, 158; foursquare badges, 158*fig*; landing page on foursquare, 158*fig*; location-based service of, 158*fig*–160*fig*; NARA Bulletin 2011-02 (published October 20, 2010) of the, 119; record keeping policy of, 18; *Records Express* blog of, 160; "Walk with the Presidents on Foursquare," 156, 158, 160*fig*

U.S. Navy LinkedIn policy, 131